The Homeowner's Guide to
Drainage Control and Retaining Walls

by Jonathan Erickson

TAB BOOKS
Blue Ridge Summit, PA

FIRST EDITION
FOURTH PRINTING

© 1989 by TAB BOOKS
TAB BOOKS is a division of McGraw-Hill, Inc.

Library of Congress Cataloging-in-Publication Data

Erickson, Jonathan, 1949-
    The homeowner's guide to drainage control and
retaining walls.

    Includes index.
    1. Drainage, House—Amateurs' manuals. 2. Retaining
walls—Design and construction—Amateurs' manuals.
I. Title.
TH6571.E75 1989   693.8′92   88-35936
ISBN 0-8306-1253-X
ISBN 0-8306-3153-4 (pbk.)

TAB BOOKS offers software for sale. For information and a catalog, please contact TAB Software Department, Blue Ridge Summit, PA 17294-0850.

Questions regarding the content of this book should be addressed to:

    Reader Inquiry Branch
    TAB BOOKS
    Blue Ridge Summit, PA 17294-0214

Acquisitions Editor: Kimberly Tabor
Book Editor: Joann E. Woy
Production: Katherine G. Brown
Cover Design: Lori E. Schlosser

Contents

Acknowledgments

I'd like to thank several people who, in one way or another, assisted with this book: Bill and Marion Dolstein, who provided many of the photographs from the water's edge; George Kiskaddon of the Builder's Booksource, who confirmed my suspicions that there was a need for this book; and Marvin Opie, who shared some of his legal expertise with me.

This book is for Susan.

Introduction

The Homeowner's Guide to Drainage Control and Retaining Walls is in some ways two books in one. On one hand, this book describes how you can build a retaining wall that is both functional and attractive. On the other hand, it discusses how you can solve water drainage problems that you might have in your yard, under your house, or in your basement. The reason these two subjects are covered in the same book is that, in many cases, they are mutually dependent. You can't build a retaining wall without considering drainage, and the solution to many drainage problems is to build a retaining wall.

How closely a wall is tied to a drainage system depends, of course, on the nature of the particular job at hand. A retaining wall can be built to help control drainage, preserve an existing shoreline, or simply as a decorative landscaping technique. For whatever reasons you build the wall, you must take drainage issues into consideration or, more than likely, the wall will not last more than a few years.

Obviously a low-lying, flat building site does not need a retaining wall, even if it is plagued by drainage problems, particularly around the perimeter of the house. In technical terms, however, the foundation of a house (whether or not a basement is present) is really nothing more than a common retaining wall. And for the most part, the techniques for designing and building retaining walls and foundations are the same.

This isn't to say that all drainage problems are solved by the construction of a retaining wall. Some are, many aren't. As you might expect, solutions to drainage problems are as varied as the problems themselves. Drainage questions can arise both inside and outside your house, above or below the surface of the ground. They may require the attention of a plumber, masonry contractor, landscape architect, and/or soils engineer.

My motivation for writing this book is probably the same as yours is for reading it. My neighbors and I had problems with our respective properties that only retaining walls and well-considered drainage systems would solve. When I began to investigate how to solve the problems, I found that there were no books specifically on the topic of retaining wall design and solutions to drainage problems. After solving my own problems, I decided to look deeper (no pun intended) into the subject and share that information with others.

In any event, this book will address many of the question homeowners will have concerning both retaining walls and drainage problems. It will describe how to build attractive, yet functional, retaining walls that will last a lifetime or more and how to effectively keep runoff water under control both inside and outside your house.

What I won't try to do in this book is provide all of the techniques involved in related, but important tasks, like mortar mixing, bricklaying, and concrete pouring. Instead, I'll focus on the design and basic construction techniques of the types of walls that most often will be built by homeowners. For books on masonry techniques, you can refer to any standard text on these subjects.

Although many authors will say that their book is a labor of love, I think you'll agree with me that there's definitely more labor than love in carrying around bricks and mortar for building retaining walls and digging trenches for drainage. Nevertheless, I have enjoyed writing this book, and as with any tool, I hope it provides you with answers to some troublesome questions.

An Overview of Retaining Walls and Drainage Systems

In the part of the country that I live—the hills surrounding the San Francisco Bay—retaining walls and storm-water drainage-control systems are perhaps more common than in many other parts of the country. There are a number of reasons walls and drainage systems are taken for granted in my area. For one thing, the area is hilly, with high ground sloping down to the flatlands at the water's edge. Second, the ground is highly unstable, a particularly serious problem considering the often acute slope of the land. Third, the area is criss-crossed by geological faults (the most notorious being the San Andreas) and is subject to a number of earthquakes of varying strength every year. Finally, the climate of the area, although blessed with moderate temperatures, endures several months of very dry weather followed by a few months of intensely heavy rains. As you might expect, this pattern leads to severe drainage problems both for homes built in the hills and for those in the low-lying flatlands.

Of course, nothing says that retaining walls are only needed on hills and slopes. A friend of mine lives in the Santa Clara Valley (south of San Francisco), where the land is relatively flat, but consists of sandy, expansive soil. Because the climate is hot and dry most of the year and extremely wet at other times, there is a lot of movement in the soil as it expands and contracts. In my friend's case, the side of her swimming pool began to crack, and the only solution was to dig up the perimeter of the pool to relieve pressure on the wall. She had a very strong retaining wall built around the pool. In this way, the weight of the soil and its associated hydrostatic pressures pressed against the strong retaining wall, which acted as a buffer zone for the weaker sides of the pool. The new retaining wall was then covered with dirt.

If the territory in which you live shares any of these characteristics—sloping and/or unstable ground, as well as drainage and watershed problems—you probably don't need (or want) to be reminded about it. One thing I've discovered (at least from the perspective of an inveterate do-it-yourselfer) is that every place I've lived—and over the past 20 years, I've lived all over the United States and Canada—no matter how dissimilar one place was from another, it always seemed that there was watershed or soil stability problems of one kind or another.

The San Francisco vicinity is particularly challenging for homeowners and do-it-yourselfers in this respect. For the most part, all of the good, flat building sites in the Bay Area were built upon years ago. Consequently, any new houses that go up are generally erected on unstable hillside lots that require extensive excavation work, unorthodox foundations, retaining walls to hold up the hillsides, and sophisticated drainage systems. On the other hand, those builders who are lucky enough to find a suitable building site in the flatlands often must contend

Fig. 1-1. Retaining walls like this one on a San Francisco hillside, are rarely built by do-it-yourselfers.

with soft, low-lying sites that are often 50 feet or less above sea level and that, consequently, have serious watershed problems.

Northern California is in no way unique when it comes to an overall lack of desirable building sites. In most cities in the country, the best building lots were developed years ago.

One of the problems that do-it-yourselfers face when encountering a retaining wall-type project is that retaining walls and drainage solutions are labor intensive. They involve a lot of digging, a lot of hauling of heavy building materials, a lot of important sophisticated engineering information, and a critical need to do the job right. There may be, at times, the need to bring in specialized and expensive heavy equipment to excavate or move heavy materials. There's no way, for instance, that the typical do-it-yourselfer could build a wall like that shown in Fig. 1-1. As a result, most do-it-yourselfers either end up building a wall that is structurally inadequate and that subsequently fails after a few years, or they end up leaving the job to a professional.

When most people think of retaining walls, they usually think of the utilitarian structures, like the simple concrete block wall shown in Fig. 1-2. As shown by the example in Fig. 1-3, however, retaining walls can also be quite attractive and play a big part in showing off a building.

Fig. 1-2. Retaining walls are commonly thought to be rather plain, like the one shown here.

Fig. 1-3. As this wall shows, retaining walls don't need to look ordinary.

Fig. 1-4. Retaining walls can also provide access to relatively inaccessible areas, as shown here.

Retaining walls can also offer additional functionality, as illustrated by the wall in Fig. 1-4, which has stairs built into it.

The retaining walls and drainage problems alluded to up to this point have generally been associated with the yard and other areas outside of the house. If you stop and think about it, however, retaining walls are part of the house as well. Take a look at your foundation or, if your house has a basement, go downstairs and look at the walls. For all intents and purposes, basement and foundation walls are retaining walls, and they present you with the same problems and solutions as a familiar ''outdoor'' retaining wall. For instance, water that collects behind a hillside retaining wall can destroy it by causing the wall to crack or literally slide down the hill. In the same sense, one of the most common problems in household basements is the control of moisture and water that leaks in from the outside. The point that I'm making is that the cause—and solution—of both of these problems is pretty much the same.

There's no hard-and-fast rule that retaining walls and watershed systems need to be talked about together. In most cases, however, they must be considered concurrently. It is a sad fact that a wonderfully crafted wall can fall apart or come sliding down a hillside if drainage concerns are not attended to during its design and construction. Figure 1-5, for instance, shows what can happen to a wall when drainage concerns are

Fig. 1-5. Improper drainage meant that this wall lasted only a few years when, with a little more planning, it could have lasted many years more.

neglected. It should be mentioned though, that improper drainage is not the only reason why walls fail. The wall shown in Fig. 1-6, for example, was probably far enough away from the tree when the wall was originally built. Unfortunately, the builder forgot that "from small acorns do big oak trees grow" and as they grow, their roots have enough strength to knock over even well-built walls.

Fig. 1-6. *Drainage problems aren't the only reason some walls fail, as illustrated by this wall that is being pushed down by the roots of a nearby tree.*

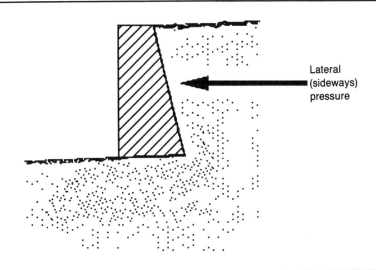

Fig. 1-7. *A retaining wall is defined by its ability to hold back the sideways (lateral) forces exerted by soil.*

A FEW IMPORTANT DEFINITIONS

Before we discuss how retaining walls are built and runoff drainage controlled, it might be useful to establish a few ground rules by defining some important terms. Let's start with retaining walls themselves.

As mentioned earlier, retaining walls are often broadly defined to include everything from masonry flowerbeds to large walls, like the one in Fig. 1-1 that helps hold up San Francisco's Nob Hill. Strictly speaking, however, any wall is considered a retaining wall if it is designed to resist the lateral (sideways) displacement of soil or other materials. Figure 1-7 illustrates this concept. This lateral pressure is created by the force of gravity as relatively unstable soil continuously tries to reach a lower level. (Chapter 3 provides a more complete discussion of soil characteristics.) Although perhaps narrower than you might initially expect, this definition of retaining walls is broad enough to encompass basement or foundation walls for houses and other buildings as well as seawalls built along lakes and bays.

Just as soil forever tries to find its way downhill, water also runs downhill. Except for those homes built on shorelines, the water that concerns homeowners most is *surface water*, which can be defined as any water that falls from the skies or rises from the Earth and diffuses itself over the surface (or near-subsurface) of the ground. This water is also sometimes referred to as *runoff*. The path that surface water takes is referred to as the *watershed*. Once surface water drains into a stream, lake, or sewer, it ceases to be known as *surface water*.

RETAINING WALLS, WATERSHED, AND LEGAL RESPONSIBILITIES

Building retaining walls and drainage systems is more than simply a matter of design and construction. Control of soil and water movement can affect you and your immediate neighbors more than any other aspect of homeownership. (This fact became particularly evident to me a few years ago, when a neighbor of mine was having problems with water running off my property and into his garage.) Legal responsibilities do not exist simply between you and your neighbors, however. There are often building codes or other legal issues you must deal with before constructing a wall or drainage system.

Watershed Liability

In the case of my neighbor's drainage problem, the circumstances had existed long before either of us had bought our respective homes. Nevertheless, it was a situation that we had to deal with, a situation that was made easier because we were good neighbors, and he knew that I had done no landscaping or excavation that would aggravate the condition. The problem was resolved by my allowing him to come onto my property to install some subsurface drainage pipes. The problem went away and we remain good neighbors to this day.

Other homeowners I've encountered have had bigger problems. In one case, a homeowner who had lived in a house at the base of a hill for a number of years had the hillside above him slide down into his backyard—some houses had been built at the top of the hill, and the developers and subsequent homeowners didn't pay enough attention to potential excavation and drainage problems. Not only was his home threatened, but the houses above him had to be vacated because of the possibility that they would end up at the base of the hill, too. Had stronger, better-engineered slope retention systems been built and a more satisfactory watershed plan installed, the problem probably would not have occurred. Needless to say, this case ended in court, and it is doubtful that there will ever be any winners.

When it comes to surface water, the law in most localities is clear about the rights, responsibilities, and liabilities of property owners. The general view is that the owner of land owns the surface water, just as he owns the land itself. Except in some urban areas, an owner of ''higher'' ground has an easement right to allow surface runoff to flow naturally from his land onto the land of lower properties. In such cases, the owner of the lower property cannot obstruct the flow of the water. The owner of the higher property may artificially drain water as long as he does so with a prudent regard for the adjacent owner's interest and does not increase the burden on or damage the lower property.

As with many areas of the law, prior knowledge of potential damage is important. The prevalent attitude is that in instances where a drain, embankment, or other drainage system has been built so that water drains onto adjoining land, the higher property owner is not liable where he had no knowledge that the drain was likely to cause damage. If prior knowledge did exist, however, the higher property owner could be held liable for damage.

The bottom line is relatively straightforward. If you have some water running onto your property from a spring or from rain, you can't simply dig a ditch and let it run wild onto someone else's property if you think it will do damage to their property or cause them problems of any kind.

Retaining Wall and Excavation Liabilities

As a property owner, you almost always have the right to excavate your land for reasonable and lawful purposes, even when you are digging close to the property line. The closer you get to the boundary, however, the more care you must take. If you remove soil along or close to the property line, you must ensure that you provide adequate lateral support during and after excavation. Retaining walls are, of course, the primary permanent lateral support that can be built.

You also have the right to grade or change the contour of your land or build a retaining wall, foundation, or embankment on your property—again, as long as you take reasonable precautions to prevent spilling soil onto your neighbor's property. If your neighbor has a building along the property line, and if your new retaining wall puts pressure against the neighbor's building, you might be liable for damages.

If you do excavate your land, your neighbor can expect that you will adhere to the "right to lateral support," which specifically applies to excavation and retaining walls. This right essentially consists of ensuring that the soil remains in its natural condition and position without being caused to fall away because of excavations made to adjoining property.

The "right to lateral support" does not take away your right to excavate your property without your neighbor's permission. Neither does this right mean that you will be entirely liable if lateral support problems occur. (A heavy thunderstorm during the excavation process can erode soil that provides lateral support.) What this boils down to is that you must be able to prove that you took adequate precautions for your own and your neighbor's well-being and safety.

Although you don't always have to get your neighbor's permission to excavate your land, in some instances you might be required to notify the adjacent property owner that you are going to start work on a job that might cause damage to his property. That notification must be accurate and complete and should be provided early enough that the adjacent owner has a chance to review your intentions.

If buildings on your neighbor's property are being put in danger because of your excavation, you might need to pay for shoring up the building, especially if not doing so will endanger your workers. As the owner of the property being excavated, you are liable for damages, caused by the removal of lateral support, to your neighbor's property even if you have hired someone else to do the work. The contractor is usually liable only when he knowingly performs shoddy work.

It is also important to note that if your neighbor has to make repairs to his retaining wall, and the only way he can gain access to the wall is by traveling on your property, you cannot unreasonably keep him off your property. And if your wall is entirely on your property, your neighbor cannot use it for purposes which trespass on your rights.

If you have any questions regarding your specific rights and the job at hand, it would probably be a good thing to consult with a lawyer, an engineer, and your local building department. Remember, damage to an adjacent owner's land caused by the removal of lateral support is actionable in court.

DEALING WITH BUILDING TRADES

Building a retaining wall or installing a drainage system is hard, backbreaking work. Although the main thrust of this book is to describe how you can do these jobs yourself, there will be times when you don't have the time, expertise, or inclination to do the job yourself, so you'll have to hire someone to do it for you.

A problem faced by many homeowners I've talked to revolves around finding the right profession within the building trades to build a wall or install a drainage system. Part of the reason for this problem is that it is sometimes difficult to identify which specific trade deals with walls and drainage on a regular basis. Masons and concrete workers are most often thought of when a wall is to be built, plumbers when a drainage system is to be installed, and landscapers when the job is finished. It's been my experience, however, that in most cases retaining walls and drainage systems are generally considered a sideline to any or all of these professions. I've known landscape contractors who have built walls and installed drainage systems from top to bottom. I've also seen cases where concrete contractors have done the same job. Except in those areas where lots of walls are routinely built or repaired (such as around a lake), few people specialize in retaining wall or drainage system construction.

What all of this means is that you may have difficulty locating someone who can build a wall or solve a drainage problem for you. For many home repair jobs, all you have to do is look in the yellow pages; unfortunately, it is more difficult to identify qualified individuals to build walls and solve drainage problems. A good place to start is at a lumberyard or landscaping supply center. As you begin to compile a list of potential contractors, ask if they have built similar projects in the past. Once you have this list of references, call up the property owners to find out if the contractor really did build the wall and if the results were satisfactory. It would also be useful to look at the walls the contractor has built. Are they still standing? Do they have cracks in them, or are they starting to collapse? Are they attractive enough for your application?

Particularly for complex jobs, you might also begin by contacting an architectural/engineering service. This could furnish you with a "one-stop" approach, because such services can provide a soils engineer for calculating soil load bearing capacities, a structural engineer to design the retaining wall, a civil engineer to design drainage systems, an architect to oversee the project, and point you to recommended contractors to actually perform the work.

One problem you may have when hiring masons to build a wall is understanding what they do and how they do it. Building trades seminars or courses might therefore be useful. What you don't want to do is hang over the mason's shoulder, watching his every move. For one thing, this will probably slow him down, and if he is working on a contract/job basis, it will cost him money. (If he is working on a day rate, it will end up costing *you* money.) For another thing, you'll probably succeed in making the worker angry.

To reassure yourself that the contractor is doing a good job, put the project requirements in writing and don't pay until the job is finished. If the job must be inspected and approved by the building department, don't pay until the wall passes inspection. If you pay for a job before it has been inspected and the inspector finds a code violation, it might be difficult to get the worker back to rectify the situation on a timely basis.

Locating qualified individuals to build your wall is a process that should begin well in advance of the time you have scheduled the work to begin. There are several reasons for this: building trades professionals schedule as much work as possible and try to book jobs weeks in advance; finding "good" workers isn't easy; and, good masonry workers are much in demand and may work exclusively for a general contractor.

How do you track down the right person to build your retaining wall? If you know someone who has recently built a retaining wall, or who has had some work done on an existing wall, find out who did the work and if it was satisfactory. You can also look for referrals at a lumberyard or other building materials supply store. Don't hesitate to go in and ask for the name of a good contractor or mason, especially if you will be doing a lot of business with a particular store. You should be able to get a list of several individuals in the community who can do a satisfactory job for you.

Finally, locate a building or wall that is under construction, stop at the site, and inquire about any concrete workers or masons who may be available in the future. If you take this approach, try to find a job that is in the early stages of construction rather than the late stages. If a job is almost over, the workers will have already lined up their next project and won't be available for a while.

Once you have compiled a list of potential contractors for the job you want done, there are a number of questions you might ask about the candidates. How long has the contractor been in business? Is he licensed, and what is the number? Has he performed the kind of work you want done? Has he ever failed to complete a job? Is he bonded? Can he supply five professional and five bank references? You might also want to find out if the contractor regularly works on residential structures or will your job be just a filler in-between his "real" jobs? Ask if the contractor intends to hire subcontractors and if he does, will they carry liability insurance.

Be sure to check references. Find out if the work was satisfactory and completed on schedule. If you feel it necessary, check with the Better Business Bureau and the state licensing agency (or whoever is responsible for licensing contractors in your area) to find out if there are any complaints against the person or company. It is also extremely important to make sure that the contractor carries liability insurance and, if necessary, workers' compensation insurance. Don't be afraid to ask for the name of the insurance agent; call up and find out if the sub has adequate coverage.

Before contracting with any building trades professional, you should get a bid (also called an estimate or quote) for the work you want done. In deciding which person on your list to deal with, get bids from each. When obtaining bids, be as specific as possible about the work you want done, and give identical information to each candidate. The most important thing of all is to make sure that everything is in writing. Don't give or accept verbal agreements.

Once you and the contractor have come to an agreement, both parties should sign a bid confirmation form and keep copies. If something happens later in the project that necessitates changing the specifications listed in an original bid, a bid modification or extra work order should be executed.

Beware of bids that are extremely low. If you hire a contractor because he is drastically lower than everyone else, you might end up with more problems than you expected. There is nothing wrong with a low bid, just find out why it is so much lower. Another way to protect yourself is to take bids on the fixed-price basis, not on an hourly or daily basis. Contract or job bids are the only way you can realistically estimate how much you will spend on the project.

In many instances, the mason or contractor will want to supply some or all of the materials required to complete his part of the construction process. When he does so, he will generally buy them at wholesale prices and re-sell them to you at retail. This practice is common in the construction industry. If you insist on providing the materials, expect for the labor costs to be slightly higher, because the contractor has fewer profit-making opportunities. Make sure the submitted bids spell out what materials the contractor supplies and what you supply.

When writing the contract, there are a number of issues that should be addressed. As mentioned above, the contract should explicitly state the method of compensation: fixed-priced, daily, hourly, etc. The contract should also state who is responsible for seeing that local building codes are adhered to. The payment schedule should also be included in the contract. Typically, there is an ''advance'' paid to the contractor on signing the contract, with additional moneys paid at the completion and approval of specified construction steps.

A detailed description of the work to be performed should also be included in the contract, as well as details about insurance coverage and any warranties and bonding. Often times, changes need to be made to the contract and, when you draw up the original contract, you should include procedures for making changes. Typical changes might involve changing the specifications, the method of work, or the scheduling of work completion. It is usually enough to simply include a clause in the contract that states the requirements for making changes. A formal change order will suffice as long as the changes are within the general scope of the contract.

2
CHAPTER

Site Considerations

Excavating means digging up the soil. Grading means leveling and shaping the soil you've previously excavated. Excavating takes place before construction of your wall or drainage system actually begins. Grading almost always occurs after the job is complete. Together, the two activities can make up some of the most backbreaking work of building a wall or installing a drainage system.

Although brute force is the most notable requirement for excavation and grading, careful forethought and planning is also necessary if an attractive and efficient landscaping system is to be accomplished. For one thing, don't begin the building process if you are unsure about the exact boundaries of your land. When you know exactly where your property ends and your neighbor's begins, that's the time to start digging.

If you will be modifying a topographically complex area, you may want to have a landscape architect or engineer analyze the site and prepare a set of plans that detail the current (and future) topographic features. Such plans would identify the various contour lines of the site as well as the flow of water (see Fig. 2-1). (Contour lines identify all points on the map that are of the same elevation.)

EXCAVATION

More often than not, the first step in the excavation process is clearing the land, a job that usually involves removing small shrubs and other obstacles before the wall can be located. If your job requires the removal

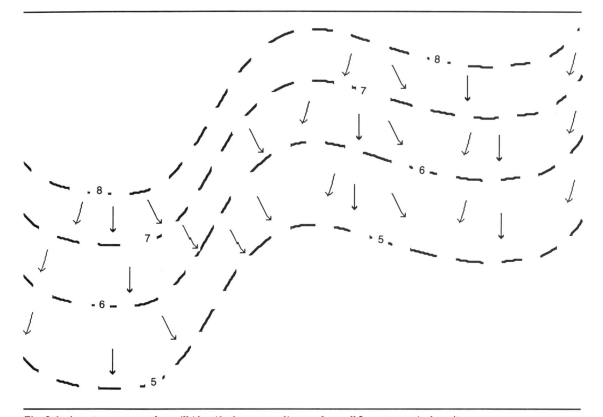

Fig. 2-1. A contour map or plan will identify the contour lines and runoff flow at a particular site.

of any large trees, be careful about cutting them down. Hopefully, the wall and drainage system have been designed to accommodate as many trees as possible. If trees do need to be cut down, check with the proper public authorities about necessary permits.

One of the basic tenets of excavation is that existing vegetation should be protected against damage. When working around trees in particular, do not dig within a tree's dripline; doing so can damage the roots and eventually kill the tree. Even if the roots are not damaged, the drainage pattern might be altered so that the tree does not get sufficient moisture to keep it alive. (Or, for that matter, the tree can cause damage to the retaining wall, as shown in Fig. 1-6.)

When the land is cleared, you should usually plan on removing the topsoil, typically down to about 3 to 6 inches in depth. This soil should not be disposed of because, once the construction is complete, it can be respread over the ground for landscaping purposes. Instead, just move the topsoil to an out-of-the-way location where it won't be tramped upon during the construction process. You can then begin laying out the building site by hammering "grade stakes" into position. The purpose of the layout process is to identify the perimeters of the wall or layout of the drainage lines. You can do this by measuring distances from known starting points and marking specific locations with wooden stakes and string.

In most cases, you will not be able to leave the grade stakes and layout lines in place during site excavation. In any event, you will always need to transfer the layout lines from the above-ground strings to the ground itself. To do so, you have two options: you can dig shallow trenches identifying the lines where deep trenches will need to be dug, or you can put chalklines on the ground in the same way that lines are put on football or baseball fields. If you dig shallow trenches, make them exactly the width of the excavation you need for the footing. If you use chalklines, you may want to use a set of lines, one for the inside of the trench and another for the outside. If you have contracted with a bulldozer operator to excavate the site, check with him to find out which method is preferable. Next, loosen and tear up the subgrade (the gravel or hard surface beneath the top soil) using, if necessary, special machinery. Remove (cut away) subgrade as required. Bring in fill material and compact it as required.

Besides the actual physical work required in digging the trenches, the greatest potential problem you face is ensuring that the footing trench is at a correct and consistent depth. That depth is determined by the local frostline specified in the building code. The entire footing (usually 6 inches thick) must be below the frost line. Assuming that the frostline is 15 inches deep and that the footing is 6 inches thick, the trench must be at least 21 inches deep.

You should monitor the depth of the excavation during digging. The most accurate method of gauging the depth is by using a transit and target pole. If this isn't possible, you can usually get sufficiently accurate results by stretching a level string across the trench opening and measuring from the bottom of the trench with a yardstick or steel rule. It is almost impossible to get trenches the exact and correct depth all around. Consequently, 3 inches, plus or minus, is generally acceptable. You should try to be as consistent and accurate as possible. In general, keep the trench level with the top of the footing.

Don't make the trench too wide. Typically, a footing is about twice the width of the retaining wall, with the wall centered on the footing. Furthermore, you'll need to leave working room on each side of the footing for concrete form boards and form stakes. If the wall is 8 inches wide, for example, the footing should be about 16 inches wide. Assuming that the two form boards (one on each side of the footing) are 1-inch wide each, and that the two stakes are approximately 2 inches square each, the total trench must be a minimum of 22 inches wide. Because you'll

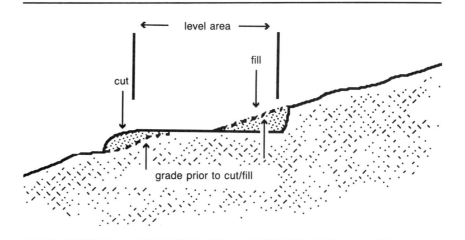

Fig. 2-2. Cutting and filling are two basic activities involved with excavating a building site.

need a little space to drive in the stakes and so on, assume that the minimum trench width is actually 24 inches wide. Additionally, you may want to bevel or slope the edges of the trench to keep loose dirt from falling back into the hole.

It is possible to dig a foundation by hand, but the work is labor-intensive and time-consuming. For large projects, it is a good idea to subcontract with a backhoe operator or owner of a trencher. If you have to do the job yourself, you can probably rent a power shovel (a combination jackhammer and shovel). Very large excavating jobs may require your hiring a bulldozer operator.

If you hire a subcontractor to excavate the site, be sure your contract specifies how large an area is to be uncovered, the depth of all trenches, and what the subcontractor is to do with the topsoil. There may be other issues you'll want to include in the contract as well.

If part of the trench is dug too deep, don't simply fill it up with loose dirt. Instead, refill the area with gravel. It is also important that the excess dirt be placed far enough away from the trenches that it doesn't get in the way or packed down.

In building retaining walls, the excavation process consists of two activities, cutting, filling, or a combination of the two. A cut involves the removal of soil; a fill is the addition of soil. Although there's nothing easy about site excavation, a combination of the two is the best approach, because cutting by itself means that you must remove the soil to a distant location, while filling by itself means that you must bring in soil. Figure 2-2 illustrates how cutting and filling can work together to produce a level area on a hillside site.

It is important to note that after the excavation process is complete the cut area is naturally more stable than the fill area. Because of this, you must make sure that you adequately tamp the earth as the fill is added.

GRADING

There are two main purposes for grading a site: to control runoff water and to beautify the landscape. Of the two, runoff control is more important, because an attractive grade that ineffectively deals with water will not be pretty for long. Consequently, determine first how you can effectively control water, then worry about how to enhance the appearance of the site.

Of course, the eventual use of the slope is important to consider. If you have a slope that normally won't be used by people, you can have a much steeper grade than that of a site that will be used as a lawn.

A slope is most easily defined by the relationship between the vertical rise over its horizontal distance. This relationship is usually expressed in terms of ratios or percentages. (Slopes can also be expressed as degrees of an angle.) To illustrate this concept, think of a slope as a right triangle, as shown in Fig. 2-3. The height is constant. The amount of change is dependent on the distance from the base of the height to the lowest point. For the purposes of illustration, assume that you are trying to gradually build up to a total vertical distance (height) of 5 feet. If the distance from the base of the height to the lowest point of the grade is 20 feet as shown in Fig. 2-4, then the slope can be expressed as a 4:1 ratio or 25 percent

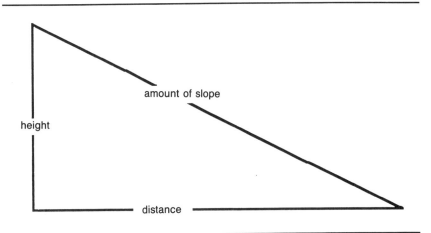

Fig. 2-3. The vertical change of a slope can be expressed in terms of a right triangle, as shown here.

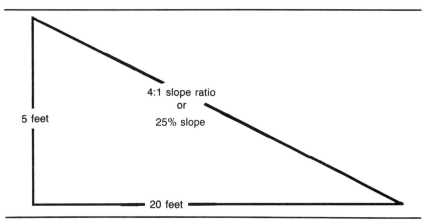

Fig. 2-4. *Expressing the amount of slope on a particular grade.*

grade. (This is, as you might expect, a steep slope.) To calculate these figures, use formulae like those below:

Percentage Method: Amount of Change $= \dfrac{\text{Distance}}{\text{Height}}$

Ratio Method: Ratio = Distance: Height

How steep should slopes be? As you might suspect, the answer to this question depends on a number of variables. It is generally recommended that you have a minimum 10 percent (or 10:1 ratio) slope away from your house. In less specific terms, a solid rock cliff at nearly 90 degrees requires virtually no slope. Stable, compacted slopes often can be as steep as 1:1 (1 foot of vertical rise per 1 foot of horizontal distance), a 45-degree angle. Unstable slopes, however, should not have less than a 3:1 ratio (or 1 foot of vertical rise per 3 horizontal feet). If you are bringing in backfill behind a wall, the slope should not have less than a 4:1 ratio. Obviously, you should be very careful when considering steep slopes and contact an experienced engineer whenever you have questions. Other general guidelines you might want to follow are listed in Table 2-1.

Table 2-1. Recommended Slopes for Typical Situations.

Use	Percentage of Slope (Maximum)
Terraced Lawn	2%
Normal Lawn	4%
Foundation Wall	10%
Grass-Covered Slope	25%
Steep Planted Bank	50%

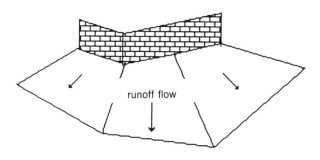

Fig. 2-5. Sloping the grade directs runoffs, but does not channel it.

Before beginning the grading process, you also need to determine the topological traits of the area you will be grading. This includes knowing where the high and low spots are, with what types of soil you are dealing, and where water can and cannot be allowed to flow. Because it is so basic, many people forget that water flows from a high point to the lowest available point along the easiest path. You can direct the flow of water along a grade, but you can't stop it. To direct it, you can use pipes, swales (channels), or obstacles to force the water to go one way or the other. You might also want to use natural objects such as large stones to divert the flow of water. You can also plan on planting grass or ground cover to diffuse and absorb the runoff. The type of cover you plant depends on the characteristics of the soil, the slope of the embankment, and the use to which the land will eventually be put.

As much as possible, try to have the new drainage pattern follow natural channels. Radical changes may not prove successful during heavy runoffs. Also try to have more than a single passage channel for runoff, because a single runoff outlet may not be able to handle the flow generated during extreme conditions.

When designing the runoff flow system, you may want to follow one of three basic design tactics. The sloping pattern, as shown in Fig. 2-5, simply directs the water away from a wall. If the slope is long enough and there is adequate ground cover, it may be possible to control runoff as the water is dispersed and absorbed into the ground. There should be some provision at the bottom of the slope for collecting and channeling runoff in extreme situations, however. Figure 2-6 illustrates one way of doing this: the land is shaped into a "funnel" so that water collects in a single point. Once it is collected, the runoff can then be diverted to a drain, pump, or basin. Finally, Fig. 2-7 shows how "valleys" can be constructed so that water is sent in more than one direction.

Grading slopes is different from excavation in that grading covers a

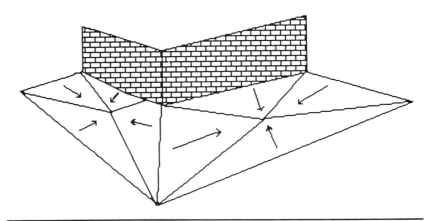

Fig. 2-6. Funneling the grade channels the runoff from several slopes into a single point.

relatively large area whereas excavation usually involves digging in a comparatively limited space. Consequently, you'll need special equipment and may want to hire a professional landscaper to do the job for you. Many simple grading jobs can be completed using a common garden tractor with a blade attached. You can then simply push dirt around much in the same way that a bulldozer or roadgrader moves soil. These tractors also have a variety of attachments that smooth, rake, and level the soil as it is pushed about. If you don't own a garden tractor or don't know

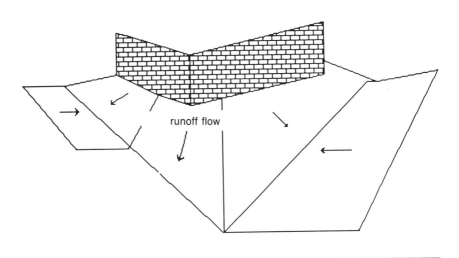

Fig. 2-7. A valley channels the runoff from several slopes into multiple outlets.

of anyone from whom you can borrow one (and you don't want to buy one), you can rent one. Remember, however, that garden tractors are designed for pushing around backfill and topsoil, not for digging out deep ditches. For big jobs that require a bulldozer or other heavy equipment, or for jobs that involve very steep slopes, you should contract with an experienced, professional operator.

Soil Characteristics

Safe upon the solid rock the ugly houses stand;
Come and see my shining palace built upon the sand!
—*Edna St. Vincent Millay*

It's probably a good thing that Edna St. Vincent Millay stuck to writing poetry instead of building houses. Still, she did realize the importance of the soil characteristics on which a structure is built. Unfortunately, most of us take soil for granted. We usually only notice it when it is tracked into the house or when our cars are stuck in it. Ultimately, however, it is the soil's attributes at a particular building site that do more to determine the techniques used to construct a retaining wall or foundation than just about anything else.

When planning a wall or drainage system, it is essential that you clearly determine the characteristics of a particular site before beginning work. If you are unable to define the important soil traits, you should contact a professional engineer who can test and evaluate the site for you. This may, in fact, be required by the local building department for those projects where a building permit must be issued.

SOIL TYPES

The geology of a site can be made up of many different types of materials, ranging from hard rock to soft alluvial soil, each with its own unique characteristics. Among the important characteristics you usually need to

Table 3-1. Soil Types and Relative Degree of Permeability.

Soil	Permeability	% of Clay	% of Silts	% of Sand
Sand	High	0-20	0-20	80-100
Loam	Relatively high	0-20	30-50	30-50
Clay loam	Medium	20-30	20-50	20-50
Sandy clay	Relatively low	30-50	0-20	50-70
Clay	Low	30-100	0-50	0-50

be concerned with are load-bearing capacity, drainage qualities, angle of repose, and elasticity.

Different types of soil have different drainage qualities. It's obvious that water will tend to simply run off solid granite, while it will tend to be absorbed into sand or other porous substances. When the ground has absorbed all the water it can hold, runoff will occur, and the water will take loose soil with it as it moves. Except in extreme circumstances, you can usually determine most of what you need to know about the topsoil conditions by simply examining the site. If the soil appears stable, and if runoff water hasn't settled in any particular spot or caused any severe erosion problems, you usually won't have too many surprises later on. Table 3-1 lists characteristics of a few common soil types, in descending order, according to their approximate level of permeability (drainage qualities).

Don't stop your examination of the soil even if you are satisfied with the topsoil characteristics. What is below the surface of the ground is perhaps even more important than the topsoil. You need to be especially attentive to building sites that rest atop landfills. If the fill material has not been correctly compacted or has not had sufficient time to settle, you may have to go to extraordinary lengths when planning and putting in the footing for a wall. If you want to build on top of improper landfill, you may be required to actually remove all of the fill material and replace it or to extend the footing down through the fill to original grade. Be particularly wary of potential landfill problems in flat, low-lying terrain. Around the San Francisco Bay (the area in which I live), for instance, land has been reclaimed from the Bay by creating landfills and then building homes on top of the fill. In most cases, this hasn't proved to be a problem, but every now and then you'll read about a foundation being declared unsafe as the house and fill settles.

When studying the soil, you need to be especially interested in its load-bearing capability and lateral-earth pressures (discussed in the next section of this chapter). In general, more retaining walls fail because of problems relating to inadequate foundations rather than failing due to lateral pressures. Foundation problems generally revolve around two issues: foundation design and the load-bearing ability of the soil.

The load-bearing capability is important because it determines what sort of footing is required for any wall that you build. If you try to build an extremely heavy wall on top of soft soil, you can be sure that that wall will crack and crumble within a year or two as the ground settles and moves. If, however, you build and anchor the same wall directly atop a bed of solid granite, it will probably remain there for years to come. To illustrate this point, consider that the San Francisco Mint (where they produce much of the money you spend) was one of the few buildings in the city to withstand the earthquake in 1908. Unlike many other buildings in the city, the Mint was built upon and fastened to a solid bed of hard rock, and the only damage to the building was to high brick chimneys. Most houses and buildings in the city, however, were built directly upon sand or alluvial soil, and these were the structures that fell apart. It is particularly interesting to note that the huge bed of rock on which the Mint still stands was moved about 2 feet south by the earthquake and that the building moved along with it without sustaining any structural damage. If the structure hadn't been fastened to the bedrock, the effect would have been much like the amateur magician's trick of pulling a tablecloth out from under a glass of water—and having the trick fail.

Table 3-2 lists some of the different types of subsurface geological beds and their approximate load-bearing capabilities. It is important to be aware

**Table 3-2. Approximate Load-bearing Capacity
of Typical Geological Beds.**

Material	Tons/Square Foot
Solid rock (granite)	100
Foliated rock (limestone)	40
Sedimentary rock (Sandstone)	25
Gravel (compact)	10
Rock (soft)	8
Gravel (loose)	4
Clay (hard and dry)	4
Sand (coarse)	3
Sand (Fine and dry)	1 ½
Clay (soft)	1
Alluvial soil (soft)	½

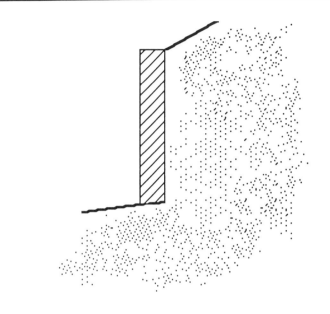

Fig. 3-1. Cross-section of a typical retaining wall.

of the load-bearing capacities of an environment before design work or construction can begin.

To understand the pressure that the foundation can exert on the geological bed, consider the following example. Assume in this instance that you want to build a wall like that shown in Fig. 3-1. The formula for approximating the pressure the foundation puts on the bed is shown below.

$$\text{Pressure} = \frac{\text{Vertical Force}}{\text{Width of Base}}$$

In this instance, you should assume that the vertical force is equal to 10,000 pounds. (This figure is deduced from what is called the *resultant force*, a value that is derived from comparing the stresses that contribute to wall failure to those that contribute to wall stability. Because this example is simply concentrating on the pressure the wall puts on the geological bed, and because the resultant force calculation is much more complicated than most homeowner's will need to concern themselves with, I won't go into it in depth at this time.) Further assume that the base of the wall is 5 feet wide. By substituting these values into the above formula:

$$2,000 \text{ lbs./sq. ft.} = \frac{10,000 \text{ lbs.}}{5 \text{ ft.}}$$

you can see that there is a tremendous force (2,000 lbs./sq.ft.) pressing down on each square foot from the wall. If the wall was 20 square feet in area, then the total force exerted by the wall would be at least 40,000 pounds. Forces such as this are common with typical retaining walls. The point I'm making here is that you can't ignore what is under the wall (that is, the foundation bed), or you run the risk of seeing even the most expensive, best-made wall crumble before your eyes.

Just as important as the load-bearing capacity of an area is the slope of the land. Some geological materials cannot support even themselves on a slope, let alone a foundation or wall. A hillside made up of granite, for instance, is "stronger" than a slope of soil or sand and won't tend to slide away in wet weather. If a steep hillside consists of sand, however, it won't even hold itself.

The angle at which geological material can support itself and be suitable for construction is called the *angle of repose*. Technically, the angle of repose is defined as the angle between the horizontal and the plane of contact between two bodies when the upper body is just about to slide over the lower. For builders, this can be translated as the degree of incline beyond which soil might not be suitable for construction without careful engineering work. Table 3-3 lists the approximate angle of repose from various geological environments.

LATERAL EARTH PRESSURE

The other fundamental force putting pressure on retaining walls is the force applied by the soil (or backfill) on the backside of the wall and at its base (footing) as demonstrated in Fig. 3-2. The amount of pressure, as well as its direction, depends mainly upon the height of the slope and the type of backfill material.

As a practical example of the effects of lateral earth pressures, look back at the wall in Fig. 1-5. This wall is slowly being pushed forward by the hillside behind it. The forces were great enough, in fact, to crumble

Table 3-3. Approximate Angle of Repose for Various Geological Environments.	Type	Angle of Repose
	Clay (damp)	18 degrees
	Sand	33 degrees
	Soil	33 degrees
	Gravel	36 degrees
	Hard rock	45 degrees

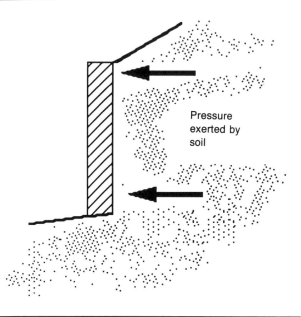

Fig. 3-2. Soil exerts pressure on retaining walls in two ways—against the back and at the base of the wall.

one of the concrete blocks in the center of the wall. Another example of a failing retaining wall is shown in Fig. 3-3. In this case, the pressure of the soil is pushing this relatively low wall into the water. When failures like these happen, there is no quick and easy fix. In virtually every case, the backfill must be removed, the wall torn down, and a new, better-constructed, wall built in the old wall's place.

When engineers design large walls like those seen along highways, they usually run extensive (and expensive) tests to determine the soil pressure at a particular site. For most walls built around the home, however, such tests are usually prohibitive in cost and often unnecessary anyway. Additionally, the amount of pressure exerted by soil against a wall is difficult to estimate because of the very nature of the soil itself.

The problem centers on the simple fact that soils consist of solids, water, and voids, and these interact in a variety of ways. (Fluids, on the other hand, do not have voids or solids and are relatively predictable in the forces they exert.) For these reasons, professional engineers can usually do nothing more than provide you with approximate estimates instead of precise details. Consequently, it may be better to "over-engineer" instead of merely meeting minimum requirements.

One important contributing factor to the pressure exerted to the backside of a retaining wall is the amount of water in the soil. Technically this water pressure is referred to as *hydrostatic pressure*. (Hydrodynamics, another type of water pressure, refers to water that flows around an object. Hydrodynamics, which usually concerns only surface water, is discussed in Chapter 8.)

Water normally exerts a pressure on a wall of 62.4 lbs./cubic foot. This pressure can be above or below ground and is always perpendicular to the surface whether that surface be vertical (as with a retaining wall) or horizontal (as with a basement floor). Hydrostatic pressures that push up on a horizontal surface are often referred to as *buoyancy*. The figure 62.4 lbs./cu.ft. should be used when you've built a retaining wall along a shoreline or a floodwall where open water is in direct contact with the wall. (See Chapter 7.)

With most common retaining walls, however, water is mixed with soil of one type or another and the load is consequently different. Hydrostatic forces are commonly measured using the equivalent-fluid pressure method discussed below. Buoyancy forces, however, are measured differently, with the main consideration being the area of the horizontal surface being pushed up and the depth it is below the surface of ground. This is of prime importance when you are building a slab

Fig. 3-3. All retaining wall building materials are subject to the pressure of the soil, including natural stone walls, as shown here. (Photo courtesy of E.W. Dolstein.)

Table 3-4. Approximate Weights of Backfill Materials.

Backfill Material	Assumed Weight (in lbs./cu. ft.)
Clay, damp	100
Clay, dry	63
Earth, some stone and sand	45
Coarse-grain permeable soil	40
Sand/gravel	30

foundation, patio, basement floor, swimming pool, or other solid concrete surface.

There are a number of ways you can estimate the backfill pressure (that is, the amount of pressure exerted by the material directly behind the wall—earth, gravel, sand, etc.). One such method is referred to as the *equivalent-fluid method*, which presumes that the backfill material has properties similar to a fluid when applying pressure on the retaining wall. The nice thing about the equivalent-fluid method is that it is much simpler than other engineering methods because it focuses only on the unit weight. (Other theories require knowledge of the angle of repose, cohension, and internal friction factors.) Particularly for small walls, the equivalent-fluid method is the most straightforward determining procedure.

Equivalent-fluid assumes that different backfill materials have different equivalent-fluid weights and will therefore exert varying amounts of pressure on the wall. Common soil (dirt) backfill has the assumed weight of about 45 pounds per cubic foot (lb./cu. ft.), while damp clay has the assumed weight of about 110 (lb./cu. ft.). Therefore, a retaining wall built to hold back a hillside made up of damp clay must be stronger than a

Table 3-5. Effective Equivalent Fluid Weights.

Soil Type	Equivalent Fluid Weight (lbs./cu. ft.)
Clean sand and gravel	92
Dirty sand and gravel	97
Stiff residual silts and clays and silty fine sands	107
Soft clay	162
Medium to stiff clay	182

wall constructed to hold back common soil. Table 3-5 lists the assumed weight of some common soils, and Table 3-4 identifies the approximate equivalent-fluid weights of typical backfill materials.

Although the equivalent-fluid method of determining the pressure that soil exerts on the back of retaining walls is relatively simple (relative to other methods), it is an engineering problem nonetheless. Every specific case is different, depending on wall design options (see Chapter 4), type of soil, surface and elevation of the backfill, and so on. The following discussion will describe one specific example. If you find that it is necessary to more strictly apply this theory to your specific case, I strongly recommend that you study a standard civil engineering text and/or contact a professional soils engineer.

In this example, let's assume that we want to determine the approximate pressure in pounds per linear feet (lbs./l. ft.) that a specific hillside puts on a common gravity retaining wall like that shown in Fig. 3-4. The formula shown below:

$$\text{Pressure} = \frac{\text{Approximate Weight of Backfill} \times \text{Height of Wall, Squared}}{2}$$

can be used to provide an approximate pressure value. To illustrate how to use this formula, assume that the backfill soil type is made up of stiff clay, with some sand and gravel, that has the equivalent-fluid weight,

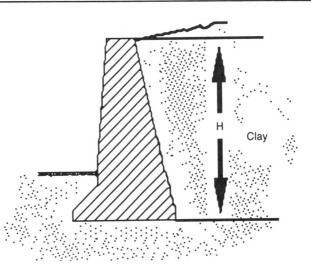

Fig. 3-4. Determining earth pressure using the equivalent-fluid method. Note that this example assumes a gravity-type wall design and a slope that does not level off.

as Table 3-5 indicates, of 107 lbs./cubic foot. Let's then assume that the height of the wall from the "heel" of its base straight up to the surface of the slope (line "H" in Fig. 3-4) is 6 feet. Plugging these values into our formula, we have this equation:

$$\text{Pressure} = \frac{107 \times 6^2}{2}$$

Solving for Pressure, we see that the pressure exerted on the walls is approximately 1,926 lbs./linear foot. This figure may then be used as the basis for helping you design the wall needed for your particular situation. (In the next chapter, I'll discuss how to use this information when designing the wall.)

Although you may be surprised at the amount of pressure the soil exerts on a wall, as shown above, keep in mind that as the height of the slope and wall increases, so does the pressure. A height of 10 feet using the same soil type will result in a pressure of over 5,350 lbs./linear foot. It is also important to keep in mind that the pressure exerted on a wall is not constant throughout the year. If your calculations make assumptions during the dry part of the year, when the soil doesn't have much moisture in it, you may have problems when heavy rains permeate the soil with moisture. The extra moisture will add weight to the soil, thereby increasing pressure on the wall. Therefore, you should also design your

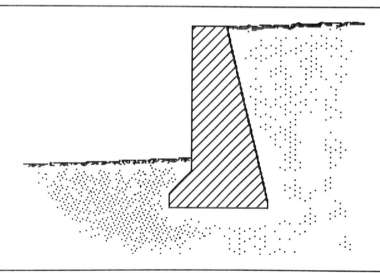

Fig. 3-5. One of the most basic ways to prevent retaining walls from sliding downhill is to place soil in front of the base of the wall on the downhill side.

plans for worst-case situations and build your wall stronger than required by minimal calculations.

The weight of the soil itself isn't the only load that should be considered. If a retaining wall is to set below a driveway, sidewalk, swimming pool, building, or other heavy objects, the pressure on the wall will be intensified, and you will have to build an even stronger wall.

It is important to take note that lateral earth pressure is closely tied to the soil bed beneath the foundation. If, for instance, you are going to build a wall on top of a soft foundation bed (clay, for example), then you should increase the calculated value of the backfill pressure anywhere from 50 to 100 percent.

Another lateral force that works against retaining walls is referred to as *sliding*. Remember that the backfill behind any wall pushes that wall forward. What keeps the wall from sliding down the hillside (hopefully) is the soil in front of the base of the wall (see Fig. 3-5) and the friction between the earth and the foundation. Base soils such as clay and silt are particularly susceptible to sliding. There are, however, construction techniques (Fig. 3-6) that can be implemented to decrease the possibility of sliding.

Yet another lateral-earth phenomenon that can contribute to the failure of a wall is *overturning*. To understand the effect of overturning, it is important to remember that the desired goal of wall design is, for the most part, to have the pressure of the backfill exerted against the base of the wall (see Fig. 3-7). In some instances, however, the direct force generated by the backfill pressure may be higher than desired and end up not being directed at the base, but at a point higher than the base (Fig. 3-8). If this occurs, the wall will be unstable and eventually may tilt over

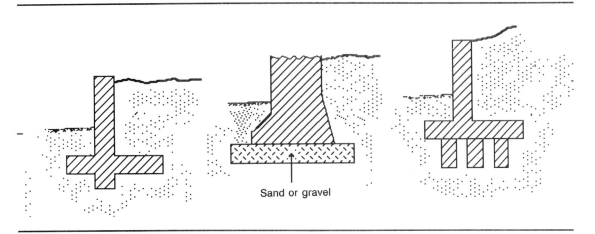

Fig. 3-6. *Other methods of providing resistance to sliding.*

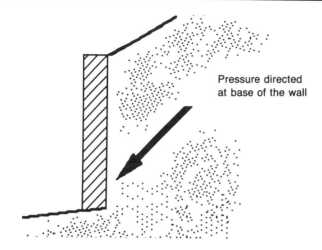

Pressure directed
at base of the wall

Fig. 3-7. The ideal goal of the design of a retaining wall is to have the backfill pressure against the base of the wall.

or otherwise collapse. The wall shown in Fig. 3-9 is a good example of what happens when overturning occurs. Notice how the wall is pulling away from the garage it was originally snug against and tipping over from the top. This is a very common retaining wall failure. This type of problem can be minimized, if not avoided altogether, by many of the design techniques described in the next chapter.

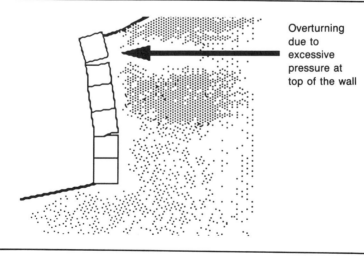

Overturning
due to
excessive
pressure at
top of the wall

Fig. 3-8. Overturning occurs when most of the backfill pressure is directed at a point higher than the base. This can be a common reason for the collapse of many retaining walls.

Fig. 3-9. This wall is being overturned by the lateral pressures of the earth .

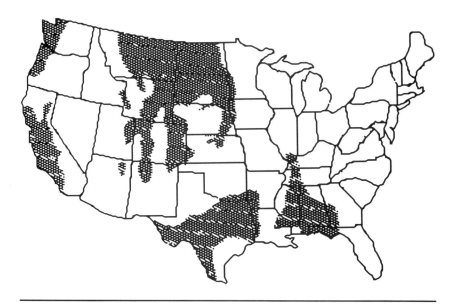

Fig. 3-10. The shaded areas of this map indicate parts of the country that are particularly prone to expansive soil problems.

EXPANSIVE SOILS

As the first part of this discussion has recounted, one of the most critical factors that determine the structural suitability of a particular site is the amount of moisture in the soil. Soil that contains, at least at some point throughout the year, excessive amounts of moisture can not only give you headaches during construction, it can literally destroy a wall once it is built.

To understand how this is possible, think of the soil as a sponge. When dry, both are light in weight and contracted in density. When water is applied to them, however, they become greater in both density and weight as the moisture is absorbed. When this occurs, the material swells, hence the term *expansive soil*. When soil expands due to additional moisture, it does so with great force, pushing outward against anything that confines it. If there is nothing there to hold the soil back (a retaining wall, for instance), and if there is enough water in the soil and the slope is steep enough, landslides will occur.

On relatively flat sites where water tends not to drain, moisture-laden expansive soils will push against anything in their way, including foundation or retaining walls. Much of the damage to walls can be averted by undertaking special drainage measures—ensuring that the grade is away from the wall, providing underground drainage pipes, and so on.

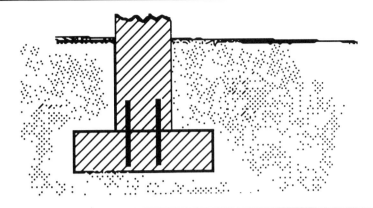

Fig. 3-11. *Potential damage caused by expansive soils can be lessened by reinforcing the footings that support the wall.*

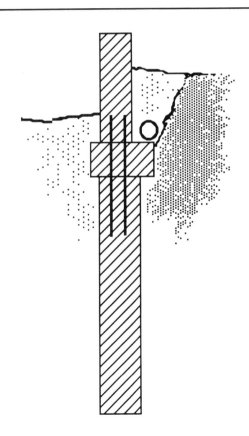

Fig. 3-12. *Drilling piers that extend into the bedrock is another way walls can be protected against damage caused by expansive soils.*

Additionally, walls and foundations may need special construction techniques in areas where expansive soil is a problem.

Figure 3-10 identifies areas in the United States where expansive soils have been a problem for homeowners. If you live in an area where the climate can be characterized as having long periods of hot, dry weather followed by heavy rains, you probably will be affected by expansive soils.

To some degree, the action of expansive soil can also be compared to the freeze-thaw cycle of ice. When water gets into cracks in concrete and then freezes, its expansive force can break apart sidewalks and highways. That's one reason why we are plagued by potholes in streets and highways every spring. Expansion of soil due to any moisture—frozen or not—is just as destructive as ice.

You can usually determine whether or not your building site is in an expansive soil area by taking a look at the ground in dry weather. If you see large cracks in the ground (caused by the excessive evaporation of moisture from the soil), you can assume that the shrunken ground will expand to dangerous levels during periods of heavy rains. When those rains occur, the cracks will fill up with water. If those cracks are next to a wall, that means extra pressure pushing against the structure.

There are a couple of special engineering techniques for wall construction that can be employed to lessen the possibility of danger to walls caused by expansive soils. One approach is to reinforce the footings with steel rebar, as shown in Fig. 3-11. This technique more evenly distributes the weight of the wall over a greater area so that no single part of the wall is affected quite so much. Another approach is to support the wall with piers drilled into the bedrock, as shown in Fig. 3-12.

Designing Retaining Walls

As defined earlier in this book, a retaining wall is any barrier designed to resist the lateral (sideways) displacement of the soil. Using this definition, retaining walls are therefore different from ornamental free-standing walls, like that shown in Fig. 4-1. Free-standing walls are generally designed only for decorative purposes, to define property lines or as a fence. As such, they don't have any specific engineering requirements other than being able to stand up under their own weight. When building a free-standing wall, the load-bearing capabilities of the soil are important to consider instead of lateral earth pressures.

This isn't to say that retaining walls can't be attractive simply because they are built to serve functional, rather than aesthetic, purposes. The wall shown in Fig. 4-2, for example, is both structurally sound and pleasant to look at. It should also be mentioned that both free-standing and retaining walls can be built from a variety of material, ranging from wood to concrete. Poured concrete is a preferred building material because of its design flexibility and structural strength. (The wall shown in Fig. 4-2 is built from poured concrete.) Wood, however, is another popular and relatively inexpensive building material, as the wall shown in Fig. 4-3 illustrates.

The main difference between retaining and free-standing walls, however, isn't in the material from which they are built or necessarily in their intended purpose. Instead, the main difference is in how they are designed and built. In this chapter, different types of retaining walls will

Fig. 4-1. Free-standing walls serve a different purpose and are designed and built much differently than retaining walls.

Fig. 4-2. Nobody ever said that a retaining wall, built primarily for structural purposes, couldn't be attractive, especially when properly landscaped.

Fig. 4-3. Retaining walls can be built from a variety of materials, including wooden beams as shown here.

be discussed; the next chapter will talk about how those walls are actually built.

BASIC DESIGN TYPES

From backyard walls built from used railway ties to very large highway slope-retention systems, there are literally dozens of variations on retaining wall design. Nevertheless, there are really only three basic design types:

- ○ Gravity walls
- ○ Cantilever walls
- ○ Counterfort (buttressed) walls

Gravity Walls

Gravity walls are designed so that their stability derives from their own weight. As Fig. 4-4 suggests, it is the massive bulk at the base of the trapezoidal-shape gravity wall that provides adequate stability. In general, gravity walls require less up-front engineering and design work and are easier to build than other types of retaining walls because, among other

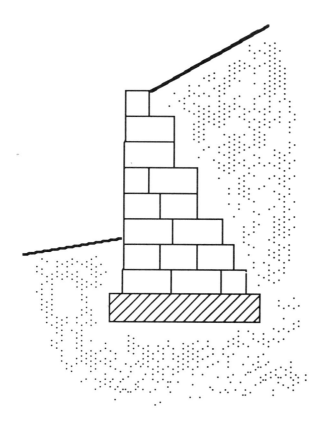

Fig. 4-4. Cross-section of a gravity-type retaining wall.

things, gravity walls are typically non-reinforced. This type of wall is often ideal for smaller projects undertaken by do-it-yourselfers. Gravity walls are commonly constructed from concrete blocks, stacked fieldstone (without mortar), stone masonry, and so on.

The two main factors that you must contend with are: ensuring that the soil beneath the wall has sufficient load-bearing capabilities; and that the width of the base is adequately proportional to the height. For larger projects, gravity walls are generally unsuitable for two reasons. They tend to cost more because more building material (concrete blocks, concrete, etc.) is required. The incredible weight they exert on the foundation is also unsuitable. You should rarely, if ever, consider a gravity wall as a viable design option if the wall is to be over 8 or 10 feet in height.

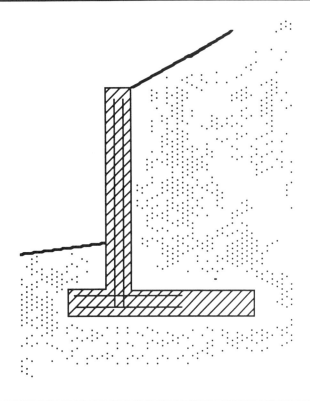

Fig. 4-5. Cross-section of a cantilever-type retaining wall.

Cantilever Walls

One of the most common types of retaining walls is the cantilever wall, like the one shown in Fig. 4-5. With this type of wall, reinforcement is inside the wall beginning with horizontal reinforcement in the base, which is then tied to vertical reinforcement inside the wall itself. Most often, cantilever walls are constructed of poured concrete, because reinforcement rods can be assembled and tied together inside the concrete form (as shown in Fig. 4-6), with the concrete poured into the form thereafter.

One advantage of cantilever walls is that, relatively speaking, they are lighter in weight than gravity walls and are therefore better suited for soft soils that have low load-bearing capabilities. Cantilever walls also provide excellent resistance to lateral pressure because the L-shaped or inverted T-shaped wall and the foundation are a single, solid strong unit working against the slope (Fig. 4-7). On the negative side, cantilever walls do tend to be more prone to sliding down a hill than gravity walls. This is due, in large part, to their lighter weight.

Fig. 4-6. A typical poured concrete cantilever retaining wall will have reinforcement inside the concrete.

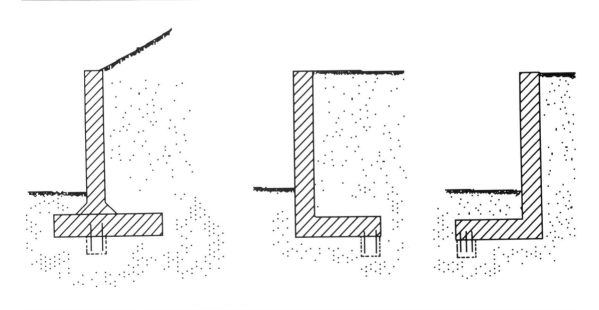

Fig. 4-7. Although cantilever walls can be designed in several different ways, they are all a variation of an L- or upside-down T-shape.

Fig. 4-8. Example of a counterfort retaining wall. This construction technique is primarily used with walls that exceed 20 feet in height. Note that the counterfort (triangular buttress) will eventually be covered by backfill.

Fig. 4-9. Example of a buttressed retaining wall. The upper retaining wall is built from concrete blocks; the buttress is of poured concrete.

Because of strength, flexibility in design, and cost effectiveness in building materials and construction, more poured concrete cantilever walls are built today than any other. They are especially effective for walls that are up 20 feet in height.

Although poured concrete is the most commonly used building material for construction of cantilever walls, it isn't the only way to build such a wall. Hollow concrete blocks are also a suitable building material, particularly when reinforcing rods have been used in the foundation and for vertical reinforcement through the hollow blocks. The hollow space around the rods can then be filled with concrete. This method makes the construction of cantilever walls possible for do-it-yourselfers who may not have the time, tools, or experience necessary to build a poured concrete wall. There are also specially designed concrete blocks available that have vertical ½-inch grooves on the exterior ends of the blocks. These grooves are designed to accept rebar. For reinforced concrete block walls, blocks like these are preferred, because you don't have to dump large amounts of mortar inside the blocks to stabilize the reinforcement.

Counterfort and Buttressed Walls

Counterfort and buttressed retaining walls are those that have external vertical reinforcement at regular intervals along the horizontal surface of the wall. If the vertical reinforcement is behind the wall, as with the wall shown in Fig. 4-8, the structure is referred to as a *counterfort* wall. If, however, the vertical reinforcement is in front of the wall as shown in Fig. 4-9, the wall is called a *buttressed* wall. In both cases, the pressure exerted from the slope is shifted from the wall to vertical braces.

Counterfort walls are usually constructed from poured concrete, because the internal reinforcing rods enables builders to tie the counterforts to the wall. Buttress walls, on the other hand, can be built from a variety of material, including wood (Fig. 4-10), and in a variety of environments, even along the shoreline of a lake (Fig. 4-11).

The buttress technique goes back hundreds of years, as evidenced by Medieval churches and other such buildings that remain standing to this day. From an aesthetic point of view, the counterfort approach is preferred simply because you don't have to look at the buttresses. From an engineering perspective, the buttress technique often provides greater resistance to slope loads.

Fig. 4-10. Buttress walls can be built from a variety of materials, including wood, as shown here.

Fig. 4-11. Shoreline walls can often use the extra support that buttresses provide. (Photo courtesy of E.W. Dolstein)

A couple of basic design concerns that you should be aware of is the spacing and thickness of the buttresses. Spacing typically varies from a minimum of about 7 feet for 20-foot high walls to approximately 10 feet for a 40-foot high wall. In just about every case, the thickness of the buttress should be at least 1/20th of the total height of the wall.

DECIDING WHICH DESIGN TYPE TO BUILD

With all of the design and construction options available, it is sometimes difficult to decide which type of wall design to build. Of course, you may already have some idea of what you want the wall system to look like—you may want a wall built from native stone or wooden beams—and that may influence your design choice. The complexity of some jobs (as defined by the acuteness of the slope, type of soil, height of the wall, amount of moisture, and so forth), however, may limit the design and material of the wall you eventually build.

When weighing various design options, there are several factors you should consider before deciding on a particular type of wall. Your primary concern, of course, should be technical: what demands does the slope you are trying to hold back put on structural requirements of a wall? To determine this, you'll need to evaluate the soil, angle of slope, and other environmental conditions. If the loads to be restrained are great, certain types of walls and building materials will be quickly eliminated.

You will also need to determine the height of the wall you need to build. Some systems and materials are best suited for short walls, while other systems are suitable for tall walls. If you are going to do the work yourself, you should also give some thought to the amount of labor needed to build the wall. Some materials (such as concrete blocks) are easier to work with than others.

The availability of certain types of building material may be a factor, especially if you want a specialty material. Concrete blocks and poured concrete are readily available, as are wooden railroad ties. Although nicer to look at, fieldstone and native rock, however, may not be as easy to find, especially in large quantities.

One factor that many homeowners sometimes forget about is the amount of space available on the site. Although a finished wall may take up only a couple of feet or so of space (at least in terms of depth), building the wall will require four or five times more space. That space is often referred to as *cut-and-fill* space. At the same time, you need to make sure you have the right to dig into the land and that you aren't infringing on neighboring property rights when you do so.

When all other factors have been weighed, you can begin to consider how you want the wall to look. If you have decided that a poured concrete wall is the soundest choice, but you have a real aversion to how they look, don't forget that you can face them with stone, gravel, and other attractive materials. (For an example of a wall with a stone-veneer face, look ahead to Fig. 5-4.)

FOOTINGS

Retaining walls stand on footings, and they are important because they support the vertical weight of the entire wall. The most commonly asked questions regarding footings are how wide, how thick, and how deep.

In general, the footing should be about twice as wide as the retaining wall, which should be centered on the footing. (In low soil bearing areas, a wider footing may be required.) If the wall is 20 inches wide, for example, the footing should be 40 inches wide. Because the retaining wall is centered on the footing, the footing will ultimately extend 10 inches on both sides of the wall. A good standard thickness for footings is between 7 and 8 inches for walls that aren't unusually tall. If the wall is high, you may want to increase the thickness of the wall.

Reinforcing rods should be considered part of the footing. Typically, rods of ½ to ⅜-inch (#4) rebar hung with wire ties approximately midway down into the trench will suffice. The rule is that no reinforcing rod should be less than 3 inches from dirt or closer than 1 1/2 inches to air. For the most part, putting in the rebar will be relatively easy. Problems sometimes

Fig. 4-12. Vertical reinforcing rods should extend from the footing and into the wall itself. Vertical rods give the wall strength and tie it to the footing.

Fig. 4-13. Not only the wall itself, but buttresses and counterforts should also be reinforced. This photo shows the interal reinforcement in the counterforts shown in Fig. 4-8.

arise, however, with bends that are required at corners and for stepped footings. Whenever a bend is made, the rod must extend around each leg of the corner for at least 18 inches (more in some areas).

If a poured concrete or concrete block wall is to be built on top of the footing, you may want to have vertical reinforcing rods that extend up into the retaining walls. The poured concrete wall to be built on top of the wall foundation shown in Fig. 4-12 will be a large wall, if the number of vertical reinforcing rods is any indication. This technique applies not only to the wall, but to counterforts as well. Figure 4-13 shows the internal reinforcement that went into the counterfort braces pictured in Fig. 4-8.

WEEP HOLES AND BACKDRAINS

An important part of any retaining wall is the weep hole that provides drainage from the backfill behind the wall. A typical retaining wall weep hole is shown in Fig. 4-14. Weep holes are usually about 3 to 4 inches in diameter, extend through the wall, and slope downwards toward the front, as Fig. 4-15 illustrates. For weep holes to be effective, a porous material like gravel should be filled around the backside of the "hole" during

Fig. 4-14. Weep holes are very important to retaining wall stability because they prevent water from building up behind the wall, thereby compromising stability.

the backfilling process. To prevent the gravel from going down the pipe, put a piece of coarse screen across the hole before pouring in the gravel.

An alternative to putting screen across the back of the weep hole is to use a manufactured drainage fabric to line not only the back of the wall, but the entire excavation before the gravel backfill is poured in. Manufactured drainage solutions also include an entire prefabricated drainage structure that eliminates the need for gravel altogether. This can shorten installation and costs, eliminate the need for heavy equipment, reduce labor requirements, and (more importantly) reduce the weight pressing against the structural slab. See Chapter 8 for more details on manufactured drainage structures.

For many walls, like the one in the above photo, materials such as plastic PVC pipe provide a suitable drain. You might also use clay tile and metal pipe (although this material can rust after a few years). And, as Fig. 4-16 shows, masonry walls like brick, block, or stone let you install weep holes without using additional materials.

Weep holes can be drilled into the wall after construction, but these tend to be less effective than holes that have been designed for proper drainage (that is, with a screen and gravel behind the hole). No matter where a retaining wall is located, you must ensure that water can drain from behind the wall. Even walls along the shore of a lake must have

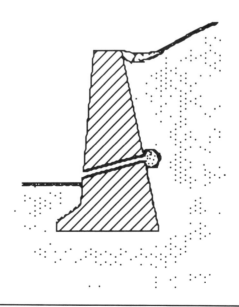

Fig. 4-15. Cross-section of a weep hole. Note that the hole should extend entirely through the wall, while sloping down from back to front.

Fig. 4-16. Various building materials provide you with different means of including weep holes in a wall. In this case, bricks are simply spaced a little further apart.

Fig. 4-17. Weep holes are necessary on shoreline walls. (Photo courtesy of E.W. Dolstein.)

adequate drainage, like that provided by the weep holes in the stone wall pictured in Fig. 4-17.

How far apart should weep holes be? That depends on the length of the wall. As a rule, it is a good practice never to have holes less than 10 feet apart. A safer practice is to space the weep holes about 5 feet apart, both horizontally and vertically.

Although weep holes drain water directly to the front of a wall, *continuous backdrains* tend to channel the water along a path parallel to the wall before disposing of it at a single point. The water is typically channeled through a perforated pipe up to 8 inches in diameter. Figure 4-18 shows a cross-section of a back drainage. This drainage method is often used around the base of home foundations.

One advantage of using continuous backdrains over weep holes is that you don't see stains on the front of the wall caused by water running from the holes. On the negative side, however, continuous backdrains tend to cost more to implement, both in labor and material, than weep holes.

REINFORCEMENT

Reinforcement refers to any material added to or any technique applied to a perpendicular wall that helps it resist lateral soil forces. The particu-

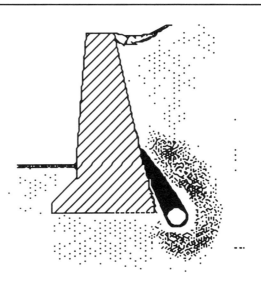

Fig. 4-18. Continuous back drains run parallel to the wall and eliminate the need for weep holes. This method of draining ground water away from the base of a retaining wall costs more than weep holes in both labor and materials.

type of reinforcement implemented depends on the type of wall being built. Reinforcement can be applied either internally (typically through metal reinforcing rods, refer to Fig. 4-12), externally (usually by means of buttresses or braces), or a combination of the two.

No matter what type of wall you build or reinforcement method you use, the main consideration is that steps are taken to make the wall stronger than the strength provided by the building material itself. In fact, reinforcement may be required by building codes in some areas. With some walls (concrete block for example) it may be necessary to provide internal vertical reinforcement, using perpendicular rebar tied into the foundation; internal horizontal reinforcement via rebar, wire, or mesh; and external pilasters or other buttresses.

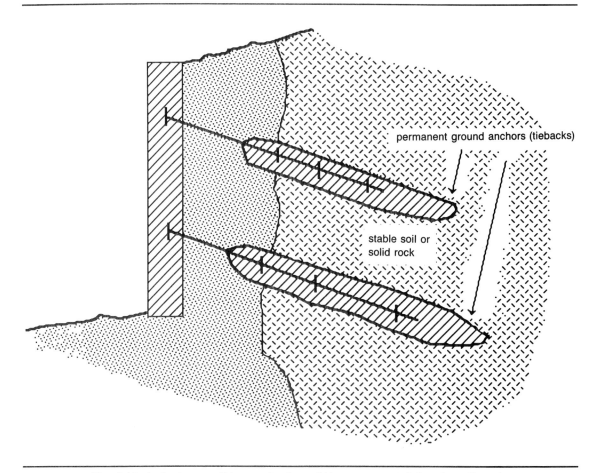

Fig. 4-19. Anchoring a wall is a good safeguard if you are worried that the wall can be pushed forward by lateral pressures.

Specific reinforcement techniques will be discussed in the next chapter when individual building methods are covered. For now, keep in mind that the design of any retaining wall must include some form of reinforcement.

ANCHORED WALLS

Once built, walls can be tied to a slope to prevent them from falling forward. This technique is referred to as *anchoring*, and the anchor itself is often called a *deadman*. Figure 4-19 illustrates one anchoring technique. Often, walls that are anchored to the hillside are thinner than normal walls. Certainly, there would be little reason to anchor a heavy gravity wall. Thin precast concrete panels or poured concrete walls are typically anchored.

In most cases, the wall will have a built-in eye bolt or other similar device on the backside of the wall. Once the wall panel is in place, a permanent ground anchor of one sort or another is put into place. A cable then forms a link between the panel's eye bolt and the anchor.

For maximum anchoring, one approach is to drill a hole into bedrock behind the wall panel, insert the cable into the hole, and fill the hole with concrete. Once the concrete has dried, the cable can be tightened. Of course, if you have built a simple concrete block wall, this might be more work than you planned or have equipment to perform. In this case, you might simply want to place a couple of railroad ties or concrete piers to serve as anchors in the excavated area before backfilling, connect the wall to the anchors, then backfill the wall.

Although it may be overstating the obvious, it is important to remember that it is better to build a strong wall tied to a solid footing than to build a weak wall and depend upon a ground anchor.

BACKFILLING

Backfilling is the process of replacing soil that was removed to build the wall. Although backfilling is a step not undertaken until the wall is completed, you must give some thought to the backfilling process early in the design phase. Specifically, you need to consider things like the type of backfill material used, how it will be applied, at what angle you can safely grade it, and what sort of ground cover will be eventually used.

It is very important that you give the concrete or mortar in the wall plenty of opportunity to cure before backfilling. The weight of the dirt being pushed against the wall creates a tremendous amount of pressure and can easily cave in or crack a newly built wall. Poured concrete walls should usually be allowed to cure a minimum of five days before backfilling begins; concrete block walls usually require three days. Once you have decided that the backfilling can begin, you should be sure to

Fig. 4-20. Backfilling should begin with the application of a layer of porous gravel directly over the drainage system (weep holes or continuous back drains).

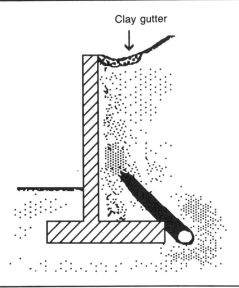

Clay gutter

Fig. 4-21. When the surface of the backfill is a relatively impermeable material such as clay, a gutter at the top of the wall may be required.

brace from the inside all concrete block foundations with kickers and studs before pushing the dirt against them. During the backfilling process, be sure to compact and tamp the soil to keep settling to a minimum.

The choice of backfill material is very significant, especially in cases where drainage is important. It is a good idea, for instance, to start the backfill process by applying a layer of coarse, porous gravel (as shown in Fig. 4-20) over or behind the drainage system. On top of that, you can then replace the soil that was removed. Finally, you might want to add a layer of top soil, especially if you are going to landscape the area at a later date.

In some instances, particularly when you need to keep excessive water away from the wall, you may want to finish off the backfill with a soil, such as clay, that has a low degree of permeability. This will cause the runoff to simply run down the slope without soaking into the ground. This also means, however, that you'll probably need to build a concrete gutter at the top of the wall to carry the moisture away, as the wall cross-section in Fig. 4-21 shows.

5
CHAPTER

Building Masonry
Retaining Walls

In earlier chapters, I defined retaining walls, discussed why they are necessary, and identified some of the problems you can face when building them. In this chapter, I'll describe how to build the basic types of retaining walls using a variety of common materials. There are a number of different masonry-based building materials that can be used to construct a retaining wall, among them bricks, natural stone, poured concrete, and concrete blocks.

As you are probably aware, bricks are an attractive building material. Not only are they relatively easy to work with (albeit somewhat tedious at times), they can also be laid in a variety of patterns and colors. (Refer to Fig. 4-16 for a photo of a typical brick wall.) Another favored and long-lasting building material is natural stone, as illustrated by the New Hampshire wall shown in Fig. 5-1 that is over 100 years old, as well as the wall in Fig. 5-2 that is nearly as old.

Poured concrete is perhaps one of the most versatile and strongest building materials used to construct retaining walls. Although the poured concrete wall shown in Fig. 5-3 (also in New Hampshire) is rather plain in appearance, poured concrete, like that in Fig. 5-4, can be made more attractive by having a thin stone veneer added to the face.

Although concrete block walls (Fig. 5-5) aren't as attractive as some building materials, they are easy to construct. Their appearance is often improved by stucco, veneer, or other such material. Yet another type of masonry material is broken concrete, such as that used to build the wall

Fig. 5-1. This natural stone wall is over 100 years old and still standing in New Hampshire.

Fig. 5-2. It would be difficult to find a retaining wall more attractive than this example of a natural stone wall.

Fig. 5-3. Poured concrete is one of the most common materials used to build retaining walls.

Fig. 5-4. The appearance of poured concrete walls can be enhanced by adding a stone veneer to the rather plain concrete face.

Fig. 5-5. Concrete blocks are perhaps the easiest of all materials from which to build a retaining wall, especially for inexperienced do-it-yourselfers. Note that wall is capped and supported in front (to the left of the steps) by a pilaster (buttress).

in Fig. 5-6. Although this type of material is concrete-based, you can use it like natural stone.

No matter what type of masonry wall you decide to build, you should plan to construct it on top of a footing. Virtually any type of masonry retaining wall (brick, block, stone, concrete, etc.) should be built on a footing. With this in mind, the next section will deal with footings for masonry retaining walls; that discussion will be followed by a description of how the various walls themselves are built. Because poured concrete and concrete block walls are most commonly built, this chapter will spend more time discussing these walls.

FOOTINGS

Once you have a good idea of where the wall will be built and have decided on what type of wall and building material to use, you should determine the condition of the subsoil as described in Chapter 3. In hilly areas that are prone to landslides or in earthquake country, subsoil tests may be required, especially if the wall is relatively large or is being built to restrain a large mass of earth. This usually means engineers must run

Fig. 5-6. Broken pieces of concrete can be used as an attractive, yet relatively inexpensive, building material.

tests to determine the soil's load-bearing capabilities. The load-bearing capacities of different soil types are shown in Table 3-1. Again, a professional engineer should be engaged if you have any concerns about the condition of the soil or subsoil.

When preparing the footing trench, don't just get a shovel and start digging. As with every other aspect of building a retaining wall, planning and care must be taken. Start by putting chalklines on the ground in the same way that lines are put on football or baseball fields. (Flour will do just as well.) Sprinkle two sets of lines, one for the inside of the trench and another for the outside.

Besides the actual physical work required in digging the trenches, the greatest potential problem you face is ensuring that the trench is at a correct and consistent depth. That depth is determined by the local frostline specified in the building code. As a rule of thumb, this is a minimum of 12 inches below the surface. The entire footing (usually 6 or more inches thick) must be below the frost line. As an example, assume that the frostline is 15 inches deep and that the footing is 6 inches thick. That means the trench must be at least 21 inches deep.

You should monitor the depth of the excavation during digging. You can usually get sufficiently accurate results by stretching a level string across the trench opening, and measuring from the bottom of the trench with a yardstick or steel rule. It is almost impossible to get trenches the exact and correct depth all around. Consequently, 3 inches, plus or minus, is generally acceptable. You should try to be as consistent and accurate as possible. In general, keep the trench level with the top of the footing.

Don't make the trench too wide, either. Typically, a footing is about twice the width of the wall, with the wall centered on the footing. By their very nature, cantilever walls tend to have wider bases than other types of walls. Furthermore, you'll need to leave working room on each side of the footing for the form boards and form stakes. If the wall is to be 18 inches wide, for example, the footing should be about 26 inches wide. Assume that the two form boards (one on each side of the footing) are 1 inch wide each, and that the two stakes are approximately 2 square inches each, the total trench must be a minimum of 32 inches wide. Because you'll need a little space to drive in the stakes and so on, assume that the minimum trench width is actually 34 inches. Additionally, you may want to bevel or slope the edges of the trench to keep loose dirt from falling back into the trench.

It is possible to dig a footing by hand, but the work is labor-intensive and time-consuming. For large projects, it is a good idea to subcontract with a backhoe operator or owner of a trencher. If you have to do the job yourself, you can probably rent a power shovel.

If part of the trench is dug too deep, don't simply fill it up with loose dirt. Instead, refill the area with gravel. It is also important that the excess dirt be placed far enough away from the trenches that it doesn't get in the way or packed down. Once the footing trenches have been dug, clean any rubble, debris, or large clumps of dirt that may be in the trenches. You do not want to leave organic scraps in the trench, or as they decay, air pockets will form and weaken ground around the base.

You should identify the outer edges of the footing by driving in stakes every 3 or 4 feet along one side of the wall. Because the stakes that hold the form boards will be on the outside of the form, set the stakes back the width of the form boards you will be using. For instance, if you use 1-by-8 form boards, the stakes should be driven ¾-inch away from the edge of footing; this should be done on both sides of the footing.

Because the standard thickness for footings is between 7 and 8 inches, 1-by-8 or 2-by-10 lumber makes good form boards. Whatever kind of lumber you use, it is important that the top edge of the form boards are straight and that the forms are level, because the concrete will be poured to the top edge of the board, then leveled off. If the top edge is not straight and level, the footing will not be level. (If the footing is not level, the wall will probably not be level.) Use a long level to check the forms as you put them up. Nail the forms to the stakes from the inside. Every 4 or 5 feet, nail an accurately measured spacer board (a 1-by-2 will do) across the top of the form; this will help ensure consistent width as the weight of the concrete pushes out from the form.

Check for vertical accuracy and, if a form board is not on true plumb (90 degrees), provide additional support by wedging "kicker" boards in at an angle to nudge the form to 90 degrees. If a form tilts inward, ensure that the opposite form board is plumb, straighten the offending board, and fasten a spacer board across the top of the form.

Reinforcing rods should be added to the footing to provide additional support. Typically, rods of ½- or ⅜-inch rebar hung with wire ties approximately midway down into the trench will suffice. The rule is that no reinforcing rod may be less than 3 inches from dirt or closer than 1½ inches to air. For the most part, putting in the rebar will be relatively easy. Problems sometimes arise, however, with the bends required at corners and for stepped footings. Whenever a bend is made, the rod must extend around each leg of the corner for at least 18 inches (more in some areas). If a poured concrete wall is to sit on top of the footing, you may also want to have vertical reinforcing rods that extend up into the walls. Figure 5-7 shows vertical footing rebars.

It may also be necessary to use a *construction joint* between the footing and the wall (this should also be done if reinforcing rods are not used). A construction joint might be compared to a concrete tongue-and-groove with the "groove" set into the footing and the "tongue" as part of the wall. To form a construction joint, simply press the narrow edge of an oiled 2-by-4 or 2-by-6 into the poured footing to a depth of about 2 inches. Remove the board after the concrete has set up but before it hardens.

After all the forms are in place, use a shovel to level out the bottom of the trench to a uniform depth as defined by the building conditions and the local code. Remember to use gravel to fill in any depressions, not uncompacted dirt. You can, however, shovel dirt against the outside of the form boards to fill small holes and add support to the forms.

Pay attention to the weather conditions and forecasts before pouring concrete. If the temperature is too cold, precautions must be taken or you will have problems with the concrete. On the other hand, if the weather is too hot and dry, the water in the concrete will evaporate too quickly, causing the footing to be weaker than normal. Chemicals can be added to the concrete to retard evaporation; you can also cover the poured footing with plastic sheets to lock in the moisture. You should also thoroughly moisten the ground before pouring the concrete. This will

Fig. 5-7. Vertical rebars should be part of the footing so that the wall, when built, can be tied directly to the footing.

keep the water in the cement from being absorbed into the earth at the expense of the concrete.

Plan on pouring the footing all at once. Do not pour part of the footing one day, then come back another day and pour some more. A "sloppy" (not "soupy") concrete mix is generally used to pour the footing. This consistency enables the concrete to fill in all corners and cavities and flow smoothly along the trench. The trench should be filled to the top of the forms. Once the concrete has been poured, use a board (a 1-by-8 scrap, for instance) to level off (*scree*) the concrete by running the straight-edged board along the tops of the form. After you have screed the footing, you may want to score (that is, make hash marks) the concrete while it is still wet. This will provide the wall with a tighter gripping surface.

Once poured, the concrete should cure for about two days before you remove the forms. Don't wait too long to remove the footing boards, because the longer they set in place, the harder they are to remove.

POURED CONCRETE RETAINING WALLS

As mentioned earlier, poured concrete is one of the more common material used to build retaining walls. Poured concrete walls are most often cantilever walls although, with some large projects, gravity walls are sometimes built.

In some ways, poured concrete walls are the easiest type for do-it-yourselfers to construct, because they allow you to actually check the work, particularly the forms, for accuracy before it is literally "set in concrete." In fact, most of the work involved in building a poured wall is up-front, in the form-building stage. This also means that if you can build the desired form, you can have irregularly shaped walls—those with curves for instance.

Setting Up Wall Forms

For the most part, the process of setting up wall forms is similar to setting up footing forms. Because walls are taller and consist of more concrete than footings, however, additional support is needed. This extra support generally consists of both kicker braces propped up against the side of the forms (see Fig. 5-8) and form ties or metal bars that hold the sides of the forms together and keep them properly spaced apart until the concrete sets (see Fig. 5-9). Form ties come in different lengths, depending on the thickness of the wall.

Of course, the first step to building the forms is to identify the location of the wall on the footing. (It should be mentioned that in some cases you may want to build the footings and walls in a single concrete pouring.) To begin, locate and mark the center of the footing. From this point, locate and mark the perimeters of walls. Remember that the wall should be

Fig. 5-8. Kicker braces are sometimes necessary to support the weight of poured concrete before the concrete can support its own weight.

Fig. 5-9. Form spacers maintain a consistent distance between form walls.

centered on the footing. If your footing has vertical reinforcing rods that will extend up into the wall, you should have some approximate idea of the center line. Once you have located the perimeter of the walls, use a chalkline (or preferably a cord and stake) to identify the lines.

Forms are usually made from ¾ or 1-inch plywood panels called sheathing, although dimensional lumber or metal sheets are sometimes used. Often, you can rent forms from building contractors or building supply centers. Because form sheathing is usually expensive (often as much as 33 percent of the total wall cost), it is a good idea to rent it if you can. Check with a cement or concrete supply company in your area to find out who rents form material. If you use plywood forms, be sure to get "good-on-one-side" plywood and face the smooth side to the concrete.

Begin setting up the forms using the perimeter lines as guides. Set up the exterior sheathing first, be sure it is plumb, and use vertical studs (usually 2-by-4s) and kicker braces to hold the forms in place and to provide support later on. The thicker the wall, the closer the studs should be to each other; the distance is usually regulated by building codes, but a maximum of 18 inches should suffice in most situations. Then, as you set up the interior forms, use a level to ensure that the two forms are the same height. Insert the form ties (these must be purchased separately even if you rent the forms) every 32 inches (closer for higher walls) as you go.

With some walls, particularly tall ones, it may be necessary to install reinforcing rods prior to installing the form ties. Some ties automatically determine the correct spacing between the interior and exterior forms; other ties require that you attach spacer bars to the forms. If the ties have wedges to hold them in place, hammer them in and make sure the ties are tight. Finally, check the interior wall for plumb and put in the interior kicker braces. It is very important that you make the forms as tight as possible. In addition to simply adding to concrete loss, water necessary for proper curing of the cement can run out and weaken the wall.

Weep holes should be inserted in the appropriate places by placing plastic pipe inside the forms. The length of pipe should be exactly equal to the distance between the inside of the two form boards. If the pipe fits tightly, concrete won't seep around the edges and into the pipe. When the forms are removed, a hole will be present in the wall.

Adding Reinforcing Rods

Poured concrete requires reinforcing rods for additional strength. Although the exact type and placement of reinforcement is generally regulated by building codes, rods typically must be ½ or ⅜-inch in diameter and hung in place with wire ties. If two horizontal rods meet at a joint, the overlap must be a minimum of 24 inches and bound with wire. No reinforcing rod may be less than 3 inches from the ground or closer than 1½ inches from air.

For the most part, putting in the rebar will be relatively easy. Problems sometimes arise, however, with the bends required at corners and for stepped footings. Whenever a bend is made, the rod must extend around each leg of the corner for at least 18 inches (more in some areas).

Oiling the Forms

Before pouring the concrete, it is usually necessary to oil the inside of the form sheathing so that the water in the concrete is not absorbed by the wood, and the forms can more easily be pulled away from the concrete. Some professional masons swear by this; others say it isn't necessary. If you have rented the forms, check with the person you rented them from to see what is recommended. In addition to a light petroleum oil, you can also use fuel oil, linseed oil, paint, or varnish to coat the forms. It is important that oil does not get on the reinforcement rods or the concrete will not stick to the steel.

Pouring the Concrete

When the forms have been erected and you are ready to pour concrete into them, begin the pouring process at the corners and work towards the center of the wall. You should pour the concrete in layers from about 6 inches to 20 inches deep as you work down the wall. Do not allow one layer to set up before adding the next layer. If you have used wooden form spreaders inside the forms, remove them as concrete fills the forms.

As you pour the second (and subsequent) layers, you should begin vibrating or spading the concrete to ensure that the cement settles and to eliminate air pockets. This is particularly important in walls that have a lot of steel reinforcement.

If you have rented a vibrator, insert it into the concrete for a few seconds, then remove it at the same rate that it was inserted. (In thick concrete, it may need to be left in slightly longer.) Vibrating the concrete too long will cause it to separate. You may also want to have someone walk along the outside of the forms, hitting the forms with a heavy hammer as the concrete is poured.

You can also settle the concrete by hand using a spade, reinforcing rod, or similar tool. If you use this method, insert the spade parallel to the sheathing, into the current layer and down into the previous layer a couple of inches. Then wiggle the spade for a few seconds before removing it.

Once a form is filled, continue adding concrete until the form is overfilled about 2 inches. Then use a screed board (a 1-by-4 will work) to strike off the excess concrete so that it is level with the top of the form. It is very important that the top of the wall be level and the concrete flush with the form.

Removing the Forms

Just as no wine should be sold before its time, no form should be removed before the concrete is strong enough to support its own weight. Under most conditions, normal concrete requires from 1 to 4 days to cure sufficiently for form removal to begin. If extreme conditions occur during that time (extremely high or low temperature, heavy rains, etc.), the form removal schedule will vary.

Form removal is fairly straightforward, involving the removal of wedges, ties, stakes, and kicker. The touchy part comes when you begin pulling sheathing away from the concrete. As with the pouring, begin form stripping at the corners and work towards the center of the wall.

If you have to lever a hammer or pinch bar against the concrete wall to remove sheathing, be sure to insert a piece of wood between the concrete and the tool so that you do not damage the wall. Do not jerk the sheathing away from the concrete; instead, use slow, steady pulls. If exposed parts of the wall requires any finishing work (smoothing, etc.), it should take place shortly after the forms have been pulled.

Special care should be taken as the concrete cures. You want to avoid excessive and rapid water evaporation from the concrete before it is fully cured. If the concrete dries out too quickly, it will be brittle. The simplest way to ensure proper curing is to simply sprinkle the wall with water for a few days. You may also want to cover the wall with damp burlap or sheets of plastic. If you know in advance that extreme conditions (too hot or too cold) will exist during the curing process, chemicals can be added to the concrete to aid in the process.

CONCRETE BLOCK RETAINING WALLS

One common building material for retaining walls is concrete blocks. Many do-it-yourselfers prefer concrete block walls, because basic masonry skills are enough to get you going. The biggest problem with concrete block walls—especially those constructed by the novice—is that they often take longer to construct than poured concrete.

Because using concrete blocks means that you will be buying prefabricated materials from a supplier, you should be aware of the many different types and sizes of blocks, as illustrated in Fig. 5-10. The most commonly used concrete blocks are the stretcher and corner blocks. The stretcher block is used between the corners. If there are three holes in the block, it is referred to as three-core; if there are two holes, it is called two-core. Because the size of the two blocks is the same, a two-core block

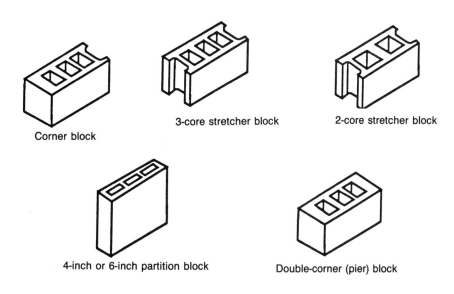

Corner block

3-core stretcher block

2-core stretcher block

4-inch or 6-inch partition block

Double-corner (pier) block

Fig. 5-10. There are many different types of concrete blocks. Be sure to get the right one for the right job.

obviously contains more concrete. Hence, it is heavier and more difficult to work with than the three-core block. Notice that both ends of the stretcher block are indented.

As suggested by their name, corner blocks are used at the corners or ends of each course (layer). Notice that one end of corner block is indented while the other end is flat. A double-corner block is flat on both ends. This type of block is generally used to construct piers or columns. The other blocks are specialized and used less frequently.

If you look carefully at the top and bottom face of each block, you'll see that one side has slightly wider walls than the other. This is because the molds that are used to make the blocks must be slanted slightly so that the blocks can be removed from the molds. When you lay blocks, always lay the thicker-walled face up to provide a larger mortar bed for the next course of blocks.

The tools you'll need to build a concrete block wall are basically the same as with a poured concrete wall. You'll also need a mason's trowel and a joint tool for laying the blocks. You may also want to get a special circular saw blade for cutting concrete blocks. You must also be prepared to mix your own mortar for laying the blocks, which means having access to water. One of the most important tools you'll use when laying blocks is a level. Have one handy and don't be afraid to use it constantly.

Preparing the Footing

There is little difference between footings constructed for poured concrete walls and those built for concrete blocks. As with poured concrete, you should plan on the footing being about twice as wide as the width of the wall you'll be using. A minimum of 4 inches should be on both sides of the wall.

Once the footing is ready, locate and lay out the exterior of the wall as described earlier in this chapter. Use a mason's cord to identify the wall perimeter and leave the cord up as you lay blocks. (A chalkline can also be used for the first course.) Each block should touch the cord as the wall is constructed. The stakes at the corners should be tall enough so that as the wall grows taller, you can move the cord up the stake. In this way, you'll be able to use the cord for reference for each course. It shouldn't be necessary to locate the centerline of the wall, although you should check to be sure that the blocks are even and have a minimum 4-inch allowance to either side of the wall.

Instead of having all of the blocks stacked up in one corner of the building site, distribute them as you'll use them around the footing. This may seem like a lot of work at first, but you'll be glad you don't have to fetch and tote while laying blocks. Also have any necessary steel reinforcement material (described below) handy.

Laying the Lead Course

The first layer of blocks is called the lead course. Laying the first course typically is completed in three stages: stringing out the block, laying out the corners, and laying blocks between the corners.

You begin the lead course by laying out a trial run of blocks, a process called stringing out the blocks. Start by taking a corner block and a number of stretcher blocks and lay them along the footing as kind of a trial run. Once you are sure you have enough blocks and that the lines and angles are square, remove the blocks, stand them on end, and evenly spread a full bed of mortar along the path where the blocks will be permanently laid. Work (or furrow) the mortar with the trowel. Take a corner block and carefully position it so that it is exactly in the corner. If the first block is not square, all of the subsequent blocks you lay will also be off.

Next, precisely position the corner block in the corner, then begin applying mortar ("buttering") to the ends of several of the stretcher blocks you will be using. Lay a pair of blocks at right angles to the corner block, one down each "leg" of the footing from the corner block. In a single motion, push the block down into the mortar bed and up against the previously laid block. When the blocks are eventually mortared together, the mortar in the joints should be ⅜-to ½-inch thick. Those joints should also be smoothed with a joint tool. It is very important that you apply an adequate and consistent amount of mortar to the block at the vertical joints. If an insufficient amount of mortar is applied and the joint is not smoothed, water seepage can occur.

At this point, you should have three blocks laid (one corner block and two stretchers), forming a right angle. Use a level to ensure that they are level and plumb. Next, lay a bed of mortar on the top of the blocks and if any reinforcing material (such as wire mesh) is being used, include it at this time.

Now begin the second course by laying another corner block on top of the first, but heading down the opposite leg of the footing so that the new block overlaps the joint on the lead course. Finally, lay a fifth block (a stretcher) down the opposite leg and mortar it in.

This completes the lay in of the first corner. Repeat this process with the other corners. When all of the corners have been laid, simply lay stretcher blocks between the corners, being sure to constantly check for level and plumb.

You should plan on adding vertical and horizontal reinforcing rods in the wall. Horizontal rebars require that you use special blocks called bond beam blocks (blocks that have horizontal indentations in them) every few layers. You can also use wire mesh or reinforcing wire as a horizontal reinforcement. Vertical rebars are simply pushed down into the cores of the blocks. In some cases, you'll have vertical rebars tied to and protruding from the footing. Use these by simply positioning the core of the blocks over the rebar and filling in the cores with concrete.

As with poured walls, you need to make allowances for weep holes or other drainage systems. Some masons think it is easier to actually build a solid block wall first, break holes in the wall for service lines when the time comes, and finally patch up the walls when the liner material has been run through the walls. It is left up to you to decide whether or not you wish to follow this procedure.

BRICK WALLS

As mentioned earlier in this chapter, building a brick wall can be a slow, demanding process. The first brick wall that I ever built, took me the better part of a summer—and the wall wasn't that big. When I later helped a friend, who was a professional mason, build a similar wall, I was amazed at how quickly he accomplished the same task. He measured the job in terms of the number of days to completion, not weeks. Since then, I've picked up many of the tricks that professional bricklayers used, but because I don't do the work every day, I'll never be as fast as a professional.

What makes bricklaying such a tedious job, at least for most do-it-yourselfers, is that every brick has to be exact in its placement, particularly

Fig. 5-11. *A single-wythe brick wall. This building technique produces a very weak wall and should never be employed for walls that are over 1 or 2 feet high.*

in terms of whether it's plumb or not. Inexact positioning of bricks not only detracts from the appearance of the wall, but can also weaken the entire structure. Furthermore, it takes a lot of bricks to build a wall; having to lift, mortar, and position each one gets old after the first few hundred.

It should also be mentioned that, although many people think bricks are one of the most attractive building materials, they can also be one of the most unstable. Bricks are usually about 4 inches in width, and when they are piled on top of each other for any height whatsoever they tend to become highly unstable. Of course, the bricks in a wall are fastened together with mortar and often with reinforcement. Nevertheless, it is not recommended that you ever build a wall over 1 or 2 feet tall that is single-brick wide. Such a wall (called a "single-wythe wall" and illustrated in Fig. 5-11) will be unstable and weak. Although a weak wall may be all right for some free-standing walls, it will be totally unsuitable for holding back the lateral pressures to which retaining walls are subjected.

For walls that are higher than 2 feet, you should plan on laying the bricks so that the wall is a minimum of 8 inches (or the width of two bricks) thick. Such a wall is referred to as a "double-wythe wall." Figure 5-12 shows the technique for constructing it.

There are several different techniques for reinforcing a brick wall. One way is to make use of vertical rebar such as that shown in Fig. 5-7. Lay the bricks parallel to each other, with the rebar down the middle. As the wall is built, a hollow center is formed which is then filled up with mortar

Fig. 5-12. Double-wythe brick walls are much stronger and more stable than single-wythe walls.

or concrete to create a solid wall over 8 inches thick. Another reinforcement method is to use reinforcing wire in between courses (or layers) of brick.

Very tall brick walls—those in excess of 8 feet in height—may require buttressing or other external reinforcement. Such a buttress (Fig. 5-13) is called a pilaster and can provide stability and resistance to lateral pressure.

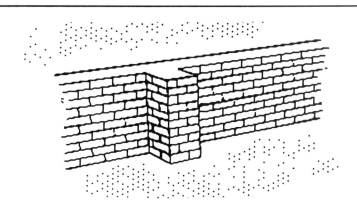

Fig. 5-13. Brick buttresses or pilasters provide stability and reinforcement for tall brick retaining walls.

Preparing Mortar

Mortar is the glue that binds. It's what holds bricks together and what keeps the wall standing upright. Mortar basically consists of four elements: Portland cement, sand, lime, and water. As a general rule, mortar used with brick retaining walls should be made up of 1 part cement, 3 ¾ parts sand, ¼ part hydrated lime, and enough water to provide plasticity. Although you can mix your own mortar, you'll generally find it more convenient, especially with small to medium size jobs, to buy sacks of premixed mortar. All you have to do then is add the proper amount of water and stir it up.

Beginners usually run into two basic problems when working with mortar: they add too much or not enough water, and they make too large a batch of mortar. Before adding water to the mixture, make sure the dry components are thoroughly blended. As you add the water, continue mixing the mortar, checking it constantly to make sure it isn't too crumbly. When a furrow of the mortar will stand up by itself, it is ready to use. If the furrow falls over, you've added too much water and will need to add more dry ingredients.

Making too much mortar is a little less critical. In general, try not to make more mortar than you can use in an hour or two. After that, the mortar dries out and is unsuitable for use. You can continue adding more water, but eventually you reach the point where it is better to throw away whatever mortar you have before mixing up a new batch.

Laying Brick

The first step to laying bricks is to identify where the outside of the corners will be on the footing. For relatively small walls, a carpenter's framing

Fig. 5-14. Brick walls can be built in a number of different patterns.

square will do. Next, use a chalkline to mark a line that connects the corners, indicating where the exterior of the wall will be. Once this is done, lay out the first course of bricks without applying mortar. This will give you an idea of exactly how they go together. When positioning the bricks, space them about ⅜-inch apart, the approximate thickness of the mortar that will eventually couple the bricks. Don't go to the trouble of measuring each spacing with a ruler; instead, simply use a ⅜-inch piece of wood to gauge the distance.

When you are satisfied that the footing, the bricks, and your original design will match, put enough mortar along the chalkline (do not cover it up) to hold four or five bricks. Take the first brick and "butter" the end of it before pushing it into the bed of mortar and snug against the footing. Butter the end of the next brick, press it against the first brick, and continue repeating the process. Continually make sure the tops of the bricks are level and the edges straight.

The second course (or layer) of bricks may need to be offset, depending on the pattern you are following. Figure 5-14 illustrates a number of

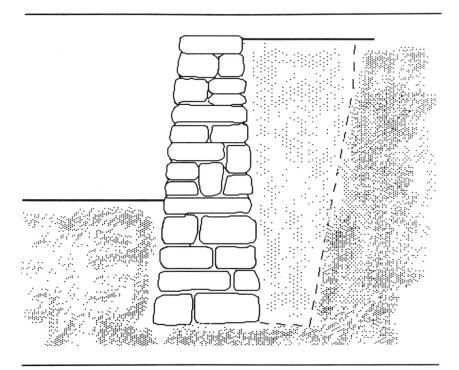

Fig. 5-15. Because stones are almost always irregularly shaped, stone walls are most often built using the gravity wall technique.

commonly used patterns. For a more detailed discussion of the ins-and-outs of bricklaying, refer to a standard masonry book.

STONE WALLS

Stone walls, like the one in Fig. 5-15, can be built with or without mortar. If the wall is built without mortar, it is referred to as a dry stone wall. In this case, selected stones are carefully stacked on top of each other, and it is their combined weight (that is, the force of gravity) that holds them in place. That doesn't mean that dry walls are as stable as mortared ones. Although there are many dry stone walls around the country, particularly in New England, it isn't recommended that you build them today, particularly as retaining walls.

Laying a mortared stone wall is not quite as easy as laying a concrete block or brick wall. The main reason for this is that, collectively, the stones aren't as regularly and consistently shaped as manufactured building material. Each stone has to be selected for its spot in the wall and, the individual stones are not necessarily interchangeable as are bricks and blocks. Consequently, it is virtually impossible to build a wall that must be regularly shaped—a cantilever wall, for instance.

Most stone walls are a variation of a gravity wall, as shown by the two designs in Fig. 5-15 and 5-16. As with any mortared stone wall, a solid foundation is important. Because the stone wall will probably be a gravity wall, and because gravity walls are by their definition heavier

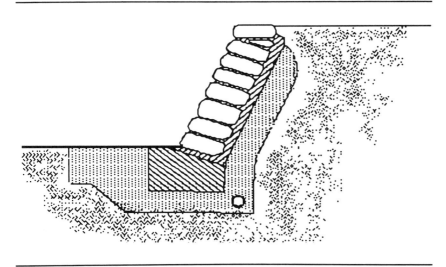

Fig. 5-16. A variation on the gravity-type wall is this ''reclining'' design. It is the weight of the stones reclining against the slope that provides strength.

than cantilever or other designs, extra care should be paid to the footing. This means that you might want to make the footing a little thicker, a little wider, or add more reinforcement.

The mortar used with stone walls is approximately the same as that used with brick walls. The one difference is that you'll more than likely need more of it, because there will be lots of nooks and crannies that will need to be filled. Because you'll be working with greater amounts of mortar, it will be easier to inadvertently produce air bubbles when laying mortar. Watch for this, because air bubbles can seriously compromise the strength of any wall.

Unless you are using a special design (like that in Fig. 5-16), stone walls should be built around a double-wythe with the center portion filled with small stones and mortar, as shown in Fig. 5-17. As the successive courses are laid, use smaller and smaller stones so that the shape of the wall naturally follows the gravity-type design.

A useful tool when building a stone wall is a ball of twine and a level. The irregular shape of the stones will make it difficult to lay the stones in a level line. As you start each successive course, therefore, you should stretch a string from one end of the wall to the other, making sure that the twine is at the appropriate height for that course and that the line is level.

With both dry and mortared stone walls, you may find it to your

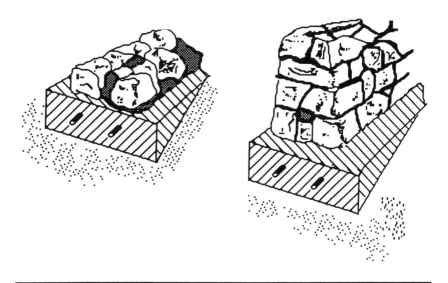

Fig. 5-17. Stone walls are often double-wythe with the center portion filled with small stones and excess mortar. Notice how smaller stones are used near the top so that the wall becomes narrower as it grows in height; this is consistent with the gravity-type design.

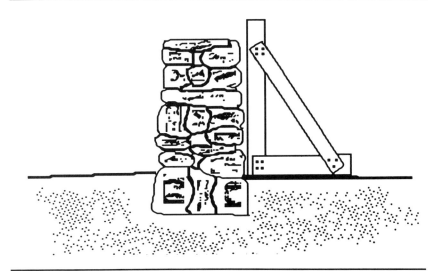

Fig. 5-18. Forms may be helpful when building stone walls too.

advantage to build a form to work against. This form, like that in Fig. 5-18, should be similar to a poured concrete form and be buttressed against the weight of the wall. A form will provide a safe and relatively easy working surface, making it easier to keep stones level and aligned. It will also take some of the pressure off the mortar until it dries sufficiently to hold up under its own weight.

GUNITE WALLS

Although gunite walls will probably not be built by many do-it-yourselfers because of the special equipment required, this method of retaining wall construction is being increasingly implemented at homebuilding sites. Gunite walls are similar to poured concrete walls in that wet concrete is applied around previously fashioned reinforcing rods. The difference, however, is that gunite walls do not have forms and that concrete is sprayed on instead of poured. In the homeowner marketplace, this technique is most often used to build masonry swimming pools. On bigger jobs, gunite is used to build tunnels and dams.

There are three reasons for considering gunite walls over poured concrete or block walls. Gunite walls are not as labor intensive as other walls. There are no forms to be built (or removed) and no heavy blocks to move around. Furthermore, it is easier to spray gunite (if you have the right equipment) than it is to pour concrete.

Second, where I live, a gunite wall costs about $6 a square foot to build (this figure does not include the footing). A comparable concrete block wall costs about $7 a square foot, while a poured concrete wall usually costs about $10 per square foot.

Third, once excavation is complete, a good size gunite wall can usually be constructed in a single day.

On the down side, special equipment is required to spray on the gunite. The process is actually quite simple. The spray equipment has two reservoirs, one with a dry mixture of concrete and the other with water. The components are pumped under high pressure (typically from 2,000 to 4,000 pounds per square inch) from the two reservoirs into a common hose where the mixing actually occurs. The gunite is then sprayed through a nozzle onto the rebar and ground surface. Figure 5-19 shows the reinforcement for a gunite wall.

Relatively speaking, it usually doesn't take much time to build a gunite wall after the site has been excavated. The reinforcing rods are tied into

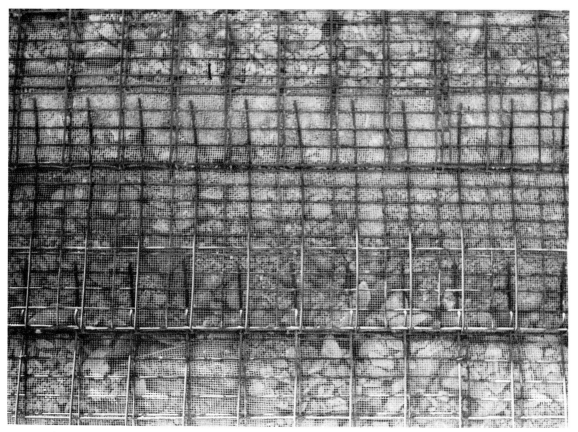

Fig. 5-19. Reinforcement for a gunnite retaining wall has been installed and is waiting to be sprayed. Note the wire mesh behind the rebar.

Fig. 5-20. Revetments are built primarily to stop erosion. This one has been covered with concrete simply as a means of keeping the rocks in place.

place in much the same manner as with poured concrete walls. The one exception, however, is that for gunite walls, you must brace the rebar so that it does not vibrate during spraying. It is also useful to place wire depth gauges at key points along the wall. The length of these wires should be equal to the thickness of the wall you want at that spot. The idea is that once the wire is covered up, you should stop spraying. Once the weep hole pipes are put into place, the wall is just about ready for spraying to commence.

Spraying is done all at once. Once complete and the wall starts to dry, a curing compound should be applied to prevent too rapid drying and curing of the concrete and the cracks that are caused by this. At about the same time, the wall should be troweled so that the surface is smooth. After that, the wall is effectively finished without your having to remove any forms or backfill any soil.

REVETMENTS

A revetment is simply a facing of stone built on top of (or parallel to) an embankment and is primarily designed to prevent erosion, not hold up the slope. Revetments are most often constructed along shorelines and are discussed in more detail in Chapter 7. This erosion control technique can be used by any property owner who has a hillside erosion problem, as Fig. 5-20 shows. In this case, natural stones were laid and the homeowner loosely covered the revetment with a coating of concrete to keep the rocks in place.

PRECAST CONCRETE PANELS

Precast panels are another building material which should be considered, although they are typically beyond the scope of the average do-it-yourselfer. These are used with the type of retaining walls that you see more and more frequently beside highways and freeways. Figure 5-21 shows a typical retaining wall supporting a roadway. Notice that the concrete panels are all exactly alike.

The reason this building material is probably not going to be used by most homeowners is that the precast panels are very heavy and require a crane to lift them into place. If you have a very serious landslide problem, however, have lots of money, and are going to have someone else do the job for you, then precast panels should be considered an option.

There are several types of precast panels that you may want to use. The type shown in Fig. 5-21 is a T-shaped panel. To visualize this, think of the letter T laying on its side. What you are seeing is the top (or face) of the T while the stem is buried in the backfill. This is what provides the wall with stability. See Fig. 5-22.

Fig. 5-21. This wall was built with precast concrete panels.

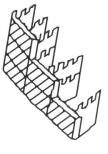

Fig. 5-22. Once a wall like that in Fig. 5-21 is built, all you see is the face. What you don't see is the stem, held in place by the backfill.

Fig. 5-23. A crib wall consists of interlocking precast components.

Another type of wall which uses precast materials is the crib wall, which is assembled much like a log cabin. This retention system consists of interlocking concrete ''logs,'' with the part of the ''logs'' you see called the *headers*, while the hidden parts are referred to as *stretchers*. As Fig. 5-23 illustrates, the headers are the horizontal concrete components, and you can see the ends of the stretchers as they back into the hill.

Precast columns and stretchers are yet another type of precast building material. With this system, columns with grooves in the sides are planted into the ground about 9 feet apart. Stretchers are then slid into the grooves of the columns and simply stacked up until the wall is built.

What is important to keep in mind about all precast systems is that you and a neighbor won't be able to simply lift these panels into place to build a wall. Heavy equipment must be brought in place to pick up and position the panels. Again, if you decide to use precast building panels, have an expert put the wall up for you.

6
CHAPTER

Building Wooden Retaining Walls

Of all the possible building materials used to construct retaining walls, wooden timbers are probably used more widely by do-it-yourselfers than any other material. One reason for this is that wood has a rustic appearance that is well-suited for many homes and landscaping schemes. Another reason why wood is favored by homeowners is that it is relatively easy with which to work. For the most part, you don't need any specialized tools, other than perhaps a chain saw and a long auger. Finally, wood walls are comparatively inexpensive, especially when compared to some masonry walls.

Wood suitable for retaining wall construction comes in several different forms—treated timbers, used railroad ties, and old telephone poles, to mention a few. When selecting wooden timbers for retaining walls, there are two rules you should adhere to: make sure it is treated with some kind of wood preservative, and be sure that it is strong enough to withstand the kinds of constant pressure soil will apply to the wood. Keep in mind that most wood retaining walls are usually about 2 feet or so in height although some well-designed ones are built up to 6 feet or so. It is recommended that you never build a wooden retaining wall over 6 feet tall.

POST-SUPPORTED WOOD WALLS

When working with post-supported wood walls, it is important to differentiate between two basic components—the vertical posts and the horizontal facing material.

The vertical posts can be of just about any tall, strong material. Steel H-beams (Fig. 6-1), for instance, make excellent vertical posts. They are readily available from just about any steel or lumberyard, come in a variety of lengths and widths, and they are very strong. Building a wall using steel H-beams is relatively straightforward. To begin, select the type of horizontal wood planks you want to use. Your primary concern here is the thickness of the timbers. A good choice is a minimum of 4 inches, although with tall walls, you may want 6- or 8-inch timbers (railroad ties, for example). When you have decided on the timbers, find some H-beams that are roughly the same width.

Next, set the H-beams in the ground. As a rule of thumb, the depth that the beams should be driven into the ground is equal to double or triple the planned height of the wall. A 4-foot tall wall, for instance, should use posts that are anywhere from 12 to 16 feet in length. If 12-foot beams are used, at least 8 feet of it should be underground. The posts should usually be no more than 8 feet apart, depending, of course, on the thickness of the horizontal material and the characteristics of the slope being retained.

Fig. 6-1. Steel-H beams, like those used in constructing this wall, make ideal vertical posts for wood retaining walls. They are strong, come in just about any length needed, and allow easy insertion of wood planks.

Fig. 6-2. Although used railroad ties are commonly used as horizontal members in wood walls, railroad rails make excellent vertical posts.

If possible, hire a professional pile-driving crew to come in and drive the posts into the ground. This will cost money, but it is worth it. It that isn't possible, use a post-hole digger to dig out the hole and plant the H-beams in several feet of concrete, following the standard rules that apply to installing fence posts. Make sure the H-beams are plumb and aligned and properly positioned in respect to each other.

Once the beams are properly in place, simply slide the timbers down the "slots." Because the timbers will not be perfectly smooth, and there will likely be spaces between each layer of wood, you probably won't need to drill weep holes. You'll still want to use proper backfill (porous gravel or other granular material) behind the wall.

As Fig. 6-2 illustrates, used railroad rails can also be used as attractive post supports. They are strong, long, relatively inexpensive (when you can find them), and are suitable for driving into the ground. On the negative side, the rails aren't strong enough for a wall much over 3 or 4 feet tall and the relatively narrow width of the rails means that you probably have to exactly cut the length of the planks. Finally, rails may be a little difficult to work with because there is no convenient way to fasten the planks to the posts.

In Fig. 6-3, used telephone or utility poles have been used as support

Fig. 6-3. Although they are somewhat more awkward to work with than steel posts, used telephone and utility poles make excellent vertical posts and can be cut with common tools such as a chain saw.

Fig. 6-4. It is sometimes necessary to add extra support to wooden posts, as illustrated by this buttress design.

Fig. 6-5. Vertical post-supports can sometimes be hidden much like counterforts by attaching the facing planks to the outside of the posts.

posts, while in Fig. 6-4 square treated posts are used. Note the external buttresses that have been added as additional support to the posts in Fig. 6-4. If you are building a wall at home, the post's height doesn't have to be exact. In fact, it is best if you plan on the posts being too tall, then cutting them off to fit (using a chain saw) at a later time.

The wall shown in Fig. 6-5 is a variation of the post-support technique in that the posts are hidden on the backside of the wall, much in the same manner that counterforts are hidden on poured concrete walls. With this wall, the horizontal facing planks are bolted to the support posts. Although it would seem that the pressure of the earth would push the facing away from the posts, the wall is a number of years old and shows no indication that it is giving way.

To further illustrate the post-support method of wood retaining wall construction, refer to Fig. 6-6. In this wall, the posts are simply 4-by-4-inch treated timbers with 2-by-10 treated horizontal planks. Frankly, it makes me nervous to think about building a retaining wall with 4-by-4-inch posts, no matter what the height is. When this photo was taken, the wall was only a month or two old, and I find it hard to believe that it won't need repair or replacement within a couple of years. On the other hand, the

Fig. 6-6. This small wall was built with 4-by-4-inch support posts. It's been my experience that walls such as this don't last very long, particularly when they must hold back as much earth as this one is holding.

Fig. 6-7. Unlike the previous wall, this one is built with 6-by-6 inch posts and, after several years, has kept a fairly steep slope in place.

wall shown in Fig. 6-7 is built with 6-by-6-inch posts, also with 2-by-10-inch planks, and restrains a much steeper hillside. This wall has been standing for a number of years and shows little, if any, wear and tear.

STACK-AND-ANCHORED WALLS

Cantilever post-support building techniques aren't the only way to build retaining walls using wood. Another popular method involves simply stacking wooden beams on top of one another, then securing them in place with anchors (deadmen). This is the technique most often employed when using rectangular railroad crossties.

An especially unique feature of the crosstie method of building walls is that, in addition to using timbers to form the horizontal facing, you use the same timbers as the anchor. In this way, you can think of the wall structure as T-shaped. Figure 6-8 provides a top view of this design method. In addition to giving support to the wall, the timber deadman breaks up the long, horizontal lines along the face and improves the way the wall looks as Fig. 6-9 illustrates.

Figure 6-10 shows a cross-section of a crosstie wall. Notice how rebar is used not only to hold the wall into the ground, but to hold the timbers together as well.

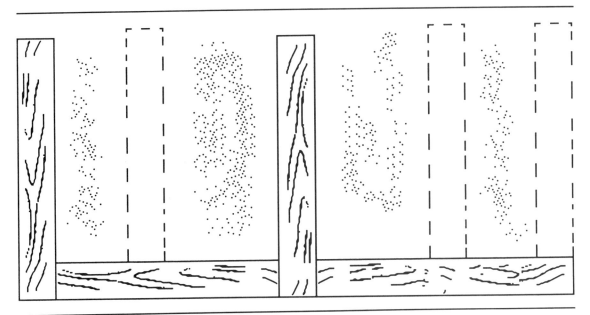

Fig. 6-8. A top view of a wood crosstie retaining wall.

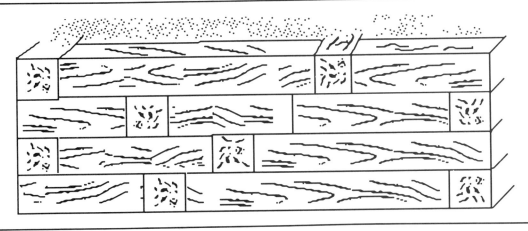

Fig. 6-9. A front view of a wood crosstie wall.

To build a wall such as this, you'll need 8-foot long crossties that are about 6-by-8 inches in size. If you plan on building the wall near edible plants or in an area where children will be playing, avoid using creosote-soaked ties; use pressure treated timbers instead. The first step, of course, is to excavate the area where the wall will be built. Level the ground and lay the first tie in place (usually at a corner or in the lowest part of the wall). When it is in place, use a ½-inch bit to drill holes about 6 inches

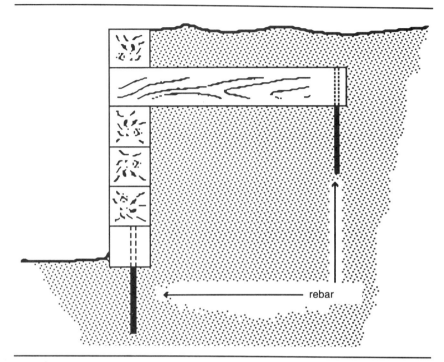

Fig. 6-10. A side view of a wood crosstie wall.

apart along the length of the tie. Then take pieces of ½-inch rebar that are at least 2 feet long and drive them into the ground through the holes. Repeat this for each tie on the first course.

Do not position the second-course ties directly on top of the base course. Stagger them about half their length so that the first-course joints are overlapped, as illustrated in Fig. 6-9. As you lay this course, drill holes through the current layer into the previous layer. Assuming that the crossties are 8 inches thick, the holes should be about 16 inches deep. Drop or drive 16-inch rebar into these holes to tie the two layers together. Each layer should have anchors, and each anchor should be about 8 feet apart. As each deadman is put in place, drill through the top at both ends of the timber and drive in the appropriate rebar. After each course is complete, backfill the anchors and tamp it in place. Be sure to use gravel along the immediate backside of the wall to ensure proper water drainage. It is doubtful that you'll need to drill weep holes, because the ties probably won't sit flush on top of each other. The top layer should not have any anchors.

A variation of the above construction method is often referred to as the ''wood beam climbing wall.'' See Fig. 6-11. This stair-step technique is designed primarily to stabilize a slope and can be quite attractive

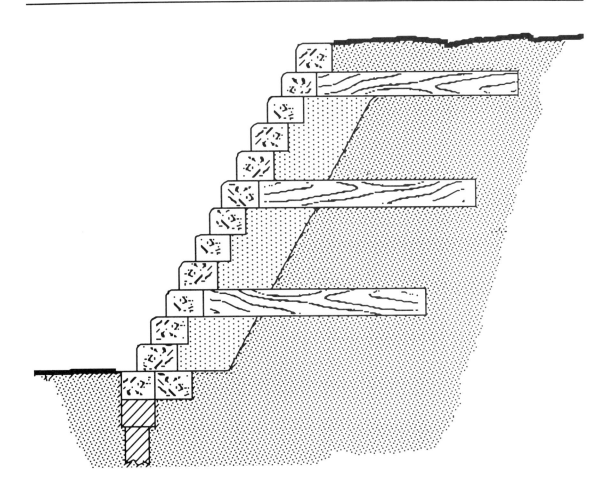

Fig. 6-11. A climbing timber wall can be built up a gradual slope.

looking. It is often preferable because less excavation is necessary. Nevertheless, it still uses deadmen to anchor the wall; spikes can be used to attach the layers to each other instead of drilled rebar.

Round telephone and utility poles can also be used horizontally, as shown in Fig. 6-12. This approach, however, requires that vertical poles be used as post-supports on the corners. This is a simple wall to build with the only difficulties being driving the posts into the ground and lifting the heavy poles into place.

Timber beams need not always lie horizontally. Posts can also be driven into the ground close enough together so that they form a solid wall,

Fig. 6-12. Round telephone or utility poles can also be used as horizontal facing members.

Fig. 6-13. Timbers can also be put into place vertically to form an attractive and strong retaining wall.

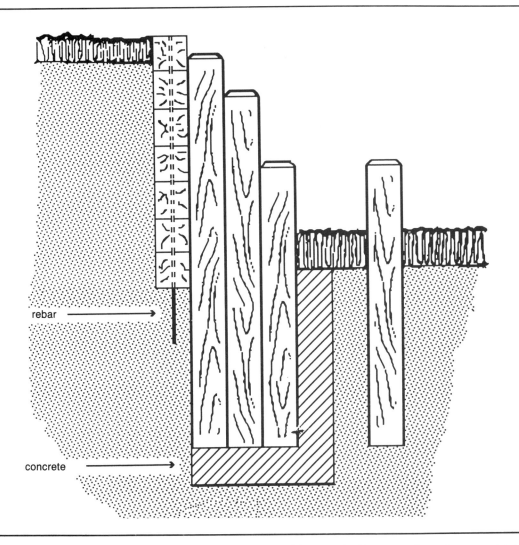

rebar

concrete

Fig. 6-14. Vertical timbers can be used in conjunction with horizontal beams to build an attractive and strong retaining wall.

as shown in Fig. 6-13. (This is how Army forts were built in the old cowboy-and-Indian movies we used to see.) The problem with this is that it takes a lot of posts, and it takes a lot of work to drive them into position. An alternate approach is shown in Fig. 6-14, where the posts are stair-stepped down. They are backed by a reinforced horizontal stack of 6-by-6 timbers.

7
CHAPTER

Building Shoreline Retaining Walls

Anyone who has ever owned, visited, or looked at a house built on a lake, river, pond, bay, or other body of sheltered water knows the importance of retaining walls. Not only do the walls help keep the hillside from sliding into the water (and most shoreline homes are built on hillsides that slope into the water), but retaining walls also protect the property from erosion at the water's edge. The conflicting forces of open water and downslope gravity pressure present shoreline homeowners with unique problems which often require extraordinary solutions, and the customary rules governing the construction of retaining walls don't always apply.

Although most landlocked retaining walls might be described as "one-dimensional" in that they generally are built to retain a slope, shoreline retaining walls can be described as "two-dimensional." This is because shoreline walls hold back a body of open water, keeping it from eating away at a slope, as well as retain the slope and keep it from sliding into the water. Furthermore, shoreline retaining walls, like that in Fig. 7-1, often fill certain recreational functions, such as anchoring boat docks and providing safe swimming areas.

To a great extent, the trends in shorefront homes and building sites reflect the general trends in standard residential building sites as described earlier in this book. The area in which I grew up—the Lake of the Ozarks area in Missouri—is a good example of this. The lake itself is manmade, created 50 or so years ago when the Bagnell Dam as built on the Osage

River. The shoreline is hundreds of miles long as it bends in and out of the coves and hills, and there are literally thousands of permanent and vacation homes built along the shore. As you might expect, most of the easy-building lots were built upon years ago. These lots, like that at which I spent my summers while growing up, were generally flat and gradually sloped to the water. Because most of these sites were quickly gobbled up, the building sites available now are less-than-prime lots on steep hillsides. For the most part, the only way these lots can be built upon is by the construction of sophisticated slope retention systems, like the terraced retaining wall system shown in Fig. 7-2. As you might expect, the building and repair of retaining walls has provided steady work for masons for many years. It was along the shores of that lake, in fact, that I got my first introduction to what it means to build a retaining wall and what it means to carry several tons of natural stone up and down steep hillsides.

It should be noted that the information in this chapter really only applies to sheltered waters such as lakes and bays. The forces of ocean waves along open coastal shores are much, much greater than along sheltered shores. Consequently, open-water shoreline retaining wall

Fig. 7-1. Typical retaining wall found on shoreline property. Shoreline retaining walls must facilitate recreational needs of property owners in addition to meeting structural and cosmetic needs. (Photo courtesy of E.W. Dolstein.)

Fig. 7-2. Waterfront lots often require both standard hillside retaining walls as well as shoreline walls. (Photo courtesy of E.W. Dolstein.)

solutions require much more sophisticated engineering and construction techniques than homeowners will normally want to undertake themselves. If your home is threatened by oceanic wave action, it is strongly advised that you contact professional engineers before beginning any construction.

SHORELINE CHARACTERISTICS

Shorelines are characterized by the landform features present where the water ends and dry land begins. These physical traits are commonly referred to as *shoreforms*, of which the basic types are bluffs, cliffs, and beaches. Note that a specific shoreline can be composed of more than a single shoreform characteristic. That is, a cliff-like shoreform can have a beach at its base.

Bluffs are steep formations, usually comprised of soft material such as sand, clay, of soft rock, that tend to be susceptible to erosion at the base and groundwater seepage throughout. As Fig. 7-3 suggests, bluffs are usually unstable, and care should be taken when building homes or other structures near this shoreform. In most instances, special drainage systems will need to be put in place so that the water does not permeate and weaken the soil. Retaining walls should be constructed to restrain the soil. At the same time, bluffs can be easily undercut at the base by wave action from the water. This "double-whammy" is what makes bluffs particularly unstable. If you are building near a high bluff, it is important that you get the advice of professional engineers before doing any work.

Cliffs are similar to bluffs in that they are steep formations, although they are usually comprised of material that is much more stable and much more resistant to erosion than the soft material that make up bluffs. Cliffs, therefore, are usually made up of sheer rock compositions that erode only over a long period of time. When they do undergo severe and dramatic changes, however, cliff-like shorelines often cause problems that cannot

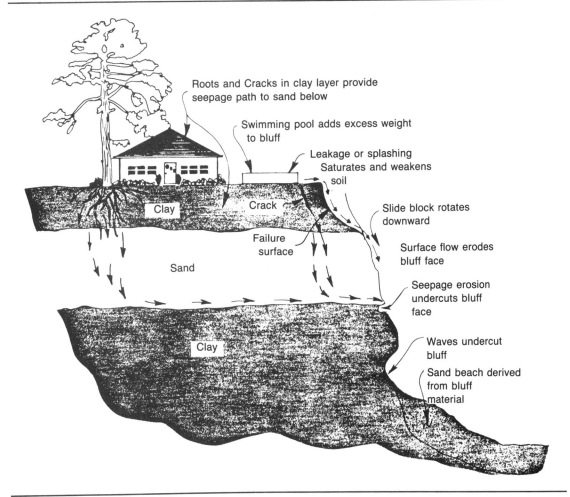

Fig. 7-3. *How and why a bluff can erode.* (Courtesy of U. S. Army Corps of Engineers.)

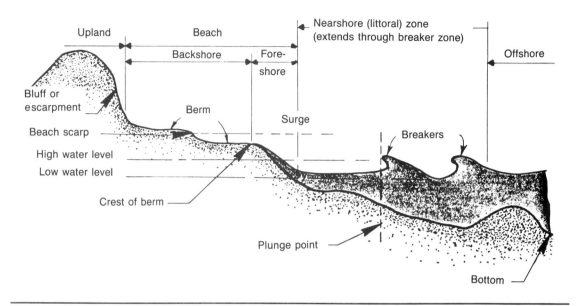

Fig. 7-4. Wave motion and sediment movement. (Courtesy of U. S. Army Corps of Engineers.)

be easily solved by individual homeowners or do-it-yourselfers. In such cases, it is highly recommended that professional engineers handle any shoreline underpinning.

Beaches are the most common and familiar shoreform. Because they generally consist of loose sediment material (silt, gravel, sand, and so on) sitting on gradual slopes, beaches are also more susceptible to the forces of water and wind than other shoreforms.

One problem confronting beachfront owners is the slow, but steady, redistribution of shoreform material. As the water level rises from waves generated by boats, the wind, tides, or simply more water from rains or runoff, the loose sediment shifts from the beach to the *nearshore*. Figure 7-4 illustrates how high-water action can take sediment from the shore and deposit in the nearshore. This means that the water just off shore becomes more and more shallow, causing problems for property owners who have boats or who otherwise want relatively deep nearshore water levels. If allowed to continue, the nearshore will eventually become dry land, and the shoreline homeowner will not have a shoreline home anymore. The proper construction of retaining walls can, of course, prevent this sort of problem.

SHORELINE PROBLEMS

As suggested earlier, one of the most common problems facing shoreline property owners is how to keep the wave action of water from carrying away the shore. In sheltered waters, wave action is usually not continuous as it is along ocean shorelines. When wave motion occurs in sheltered waters, it is usually because of passing boats or the wind. Each time a wave breaks on the shore, it runs up the slope as far as it can, then retreats back down the slope. With each retreat, the wave takes a little of the shore material with it. In technical terms, this material is referred to as *litteral drift*.

Few, if any, waves hit the shore perpendicularly. Instead, they reach the shore at an angle. Consequently, the sediment being transported by the wave does not move out to the nearshore in a straight line. Rather, it moves in a zigzag path as it goes offshore, onshore, offshore, and so on, along the shoreline.

In addition to waves, seasonal factors—rain, ice, runoff, etc.—can play a part in shoreline control problems as well. Ice in particular is important because it can break apart shorelines and cause havoc with retaining walls, docks, boats, or anything else with which it comes in contact.

The upshot of this is that shoreline property owners who do not take steps to control their shoreline can be faced with the nuisance of water that is not deep enough for navigation or recreation. More serious is the fact that they can also lose shorefront property as it is slowly eroded away. A 10,000 square foot lot, for example, can become 9,000 square foot lot in the matter of a few years.

SHORELINE SOLUTIONS

The shoreline solution you elect to implement depends, of course, on the type of problem with which you are faced. There are a number of common solutions, ranging from those that completely separate the water from the land to those that simply absorb wave motion so that there is less wear and tear on the shore.

Shoreline Wall Design Considerations

No matter what type of shoreline wall you eventually build, there are several factors all shoreline walls have in common. For one thing, you need to be concerned about the soil in front of the wall as well as behind it, particularly at the base or toe of the wall. Lack of adequate toe support is one of the main reasons shoreline retaining walls fail, especially in areas of relatively strong wave action. Figure 7-5 illustrates what happens when toe support is not provided. The water comes into the wall, then swirls down and returns to the main body of water, taking soil at the toe with it. The water will continue to erode at the toe until there is not enough support for the wall, and it will collapse. To counteract this, it is necessary to put large rocks in place at the toe of the wall to prevent the sediment from washing away.

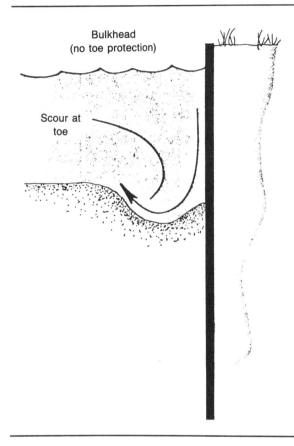

Fig. 7-5. The base or toe of shoreline retaining walls needs to be protected from erosion. (Courtesy of U. S. Army Corps of Engineers.)

You must also take care to provide adequate filtering with shoreline walls. As Fig. 7-6 illustrates, filtering is accomplished by putting a special filter cloth (see Chapter 8 for a more detailed description of this filtering cloth or check with the District Engineer at your local U.S. Army Corp of Engineers for a list of such products) or a layer of porous stones under the toe support and other large rocks that protect sediment. If filtering steps aren't implemented, the sediment will eventually come up between the large rocks, and they will be covered up by it.

Backfill material for all shoreline walls should be carefully selected. In general, use only granular, porous material. Avoid using nonporous, clay-based materials.

Post-Supported Seawalls and Bulkheads

The most commonly implemented shoreline solutions are the *seawall* and *bulkhead*. In technical terms, seawalls and bulkheads are not the same, although the names are commonly interchanged. The difference between

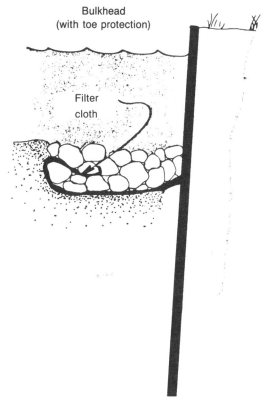

Bulkhead
(with toe protection)

Filter
cloth

Fig. 7-6. Anywhere large rocks are used for erosion protection, proper filtering techniques must be employed to prevent settling and erosion. (Courtesy of U. S. Army Corps of Engineers.)

the two is that seawalls are built to keep the water from eating into the land, while bulkheads are built to keep the land from sliding into the water. The reason the terms have generally become synomous is that a single wall is often built to serve both functions. The wall system shown in Fig. 7-7 illustrates this. The wall at the edge of the water is a seawall, although it is also holding back the soil on the slope behind it. For most situations, the terms can be used interchangeably and will be in this discussion.

Several different materials and techniques can be used to build seawalls. Among the materials are steel and aluminum sheet metal, treated timber beams, sand bags, used automobile tires, natural stone, and poured concrete. The selection of building material depends upon the type of problem you are trying to solve, cost, appearance, and availability of building materials.

To illustrate how bulkheads might be used, consider the problem Sherry, a friend of mine, had to deal with several years ago. Sherry owned a weekend/vacation home on a comparatively new (less than 20 years) manmade lake in Texas. Although her house was on an extremely flat lot, it was built upon relatively soft soil and was highly susceptible to erosion. After a couple of years, in fact, the lake took away nearly 10 feet of her lot. It became apparent to her that something needed to be done and fairly quickly. Sherry's solution was to build a relatively inexpensive (yet labor-intensive) bulkhead out of used tires. This tactic accomplished three things: it enabled her to stave off the natural tendencies of the water to erode the land, it reclaimed the land she had lost, and it made it possible for her to actually enlarge the effective size of her lot when she built the bulkhead out beyond the original shoreline.

The way she went about building the wall was to first contact the appropriate authorities, including the U.S. Army Corp of Engineers, as well as her neighbors, to find out what she could and couldn't do. She then made her plans and started construction in the winter, when the lake was at its lowest level.

The first step, and most expensive, was to have a company come in and drive telephone pole-like pilings into the ground about 3 feet apart out beyond her existing shoreline. The pilings were pounded several feet deep into the ground and protruded up several feet so that the tops of the posts were about level with the elevation of her lot. Once these pilings

Fig. 7-7. Retaining walls built along the shore hold back the soil on one side and the water on the other. (Photo courtesy of E.W. Dolstein.)

were in place, she began the arduous task of collecting and hauling used tires to the lake. During the week, she would go to nearby gas stations in her North Dallas neighborhood and get whatever used tires they were going to throw away. On Saturdays, she would take these up to the lake (pulling a rental trailer behind her car) where she would drop the tires over the pilings. As she went from piling to piling, she would fasten the side-by-side tires together using heavy wire.

When all of the pilings had tires stacked to the top, Sherry then began bringing in rocks, which she dropped into the center of each stack of tires. After that, she had a few truckloads of rocks and other granular, porous material delivered to be dumped in as backfill. Finally, a few truckloads of top soil was used to cover and level the lot. In addition to providing for land retention and reclamation, the wall gave Sherry a convenient docking structure that she didn't have before.

It should be mentioned that bulkheads like the one Sherry built shield only the land directly behind them and, in some cases, may actually lead

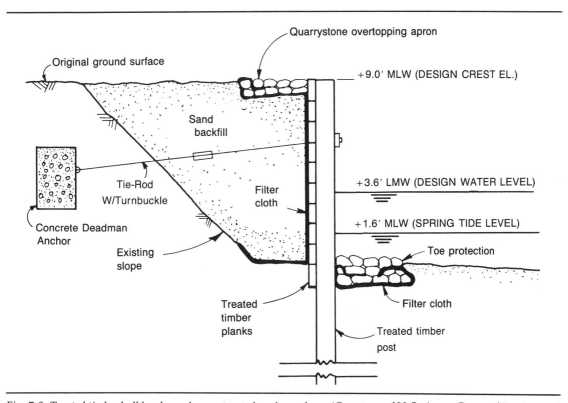

Fig. 7-8. Treated timber bulkheads can be constructed as shown here. (Courtesy of U.S. Army Corps of Engineers.)

to increased erosion on adjoining, unprotected areas. This means that if you have plans to build such a structure, be sure you let those property owners who may be adversely affected know about your plans.

Treated timber is a more commonly used bulkhead building material, as Fig. 7-8 illustrates. In this example, a concrete deadman is used to anchor the wall. Note that the anchor is firmly seated in the original soil, not the backfill. Typically, the treated timber vertical posts are 12-by-12 inches in size and of varying height (a 9-foot high bluff should use vertical posts 24 feet long). They are spaced no more than 6 feet apart. The horizontal planks, on the other hand, should be about 3-by-12 inches in size and about 12 feet long. When drilling holes into timber for the anchor, make sure that the bolt holes are no larger than $\frac{1}{16}$-inch greater than the bolt itself. Use only protected, rustproof hardware (bolts, nuts, turnbuckles, etc.).

It is recommended that a filter cloth be applied to the backside of the timber bulkheads. This is to prevent sand and other backfill material from washing away because of the slight spaces between the planks. On the plus side, these spaces mean that weep holes are unnecessary. Filter cloth is also included underneath the rocks used as toe support at the base of the wall. This is to prevent the rocks from settling into the bottom. The stone at the top of the wall is there for appearance as well as to prevent erosion of backfill if waves come over the top of the wall.

In general, post-supported bulkheads (like the used-tire wall or the treated timber bulkhead described above) should be used where wave height is less than 5 feet. One of the nice things about post-supported bulkheads, as Sherry proved, is that once the posts are put in place (usually by a professional crew), the wall can be finished by a do-it-yourselfer. Furthermore, post-supported walls can be relatively inexpensive, once the posts themselves are paid for.

There are several other types of post-supported walls in addition to those described above. An effective and inexpensive, although unattractive, wall is a hogwire fence backed by sandbags. In this case, posts are driven into the ground, mesh-wire fencing is attached to the land-side of the posts, and sandbags are stacked behind the fence. As the wire rusts and the bags tear, this wall becomes increasingly ugly. Because it is quick to erect, however, it may be fine, especially in emergency situations.

Sheet metal—steel or aluminum—is the type of bulkhead building material used to solve serious shoreline problems. By serious, I mean that if your shore is being battered by waves that are 5 feet or greater in height, you should consider having a heavy sheet metal bulkhead built, like that in Fig. 7-9. This typically isn't the type of wall you can build yourself, because it requires trained personnel and special pile-driving equipment. The heavy, tall sheets of metal (some up to 12 feet tall) are literally

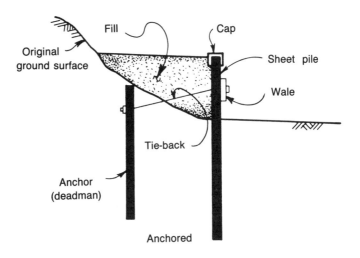

Fig. 7-9. Sheet metal bulkheads are typically either steel or aluminum and can be cantilevered or anchored in design. (Courtesy of U. S. Army Corps of Engineers.)

pounded into the ground just as you would drive a fence post into the soil. Because cantilever bulkheads like that in Fig. 7-9 are self-supporting, they usually need to be driven into the ground to a depth equal to half to two-thirds of their total height. That is, a 12 foot tall piece of metal should sit from 6 to 8 feet below the surface. If you use shorter pieces of sheet metal, you might need to anchor it, also shown in Fig. 7-9.

Another type of post-supported bulkhead is the steel H-pile and timber wall. In this case, steel H-beams are used as posts, driven into the ground. Once in place, railroad ties or other treated timbers are slid between the flanges of the H-beams as shown in Fig. 7-10. This makes an attractive wall which can be used in non-shoreline applications as well.

Revetments

Although they are not by definition retaining walls, revetments should be mentioned because they can be a solution to many shoreline problems. Basically, a revetment is simply a solid facing (concrete, stone, etc.) constructed to protect the shore from being eroded by water. The difference between a retaining wall and a revetment is that a retaining wall, for practical purposes, is considered to be perpendicular to the surface. Revetments, on the other hand, are built parallel to the surface and can be built for gradual slopes. A typical revetment is shown in Fig. 5-20. Revetments should not be used where wave action is greater than 5 feet.

Fig. 7-10. Steel H-beams make good posts. Planks can be treated timber as shown here or even used railroad ties.

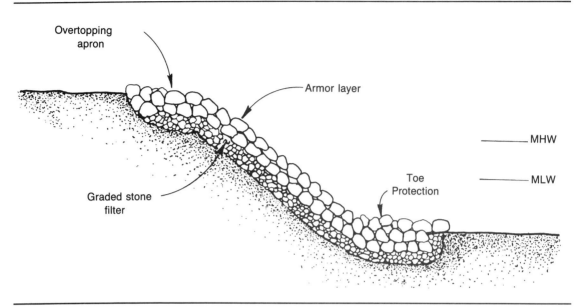

Fig. 7-11. Cross-section of a typical natural stone revetment. (Courtesy of U. S. Army Corps of Engineers.)

As Fig. 7-11 illustrates, revetments are made up of three parts, toe support, armor, and a filter layer. The armor can be any of a number of materials, from natural rock to concrete rubble to sand bags. The filter layer allows drainage and keeps the armor from washing away. The toe support keeps the base of the wall from washing away.

Special mention should be made of the filter layer. For this layer, you should use a specially designed erosion control fabric that has soil retention and hydraulic properties and is resistant to soil clogging. The material must also be exceptionally strong and should meet U.S. Army Corp of Engineer specifications. These fabrics will be discussed in Chapter 8. Mirafi Inc. (Charlotte, NC) produces a number of fabrics designed for specific applications. Additionally, there are several types of specialized revetment materials, including nylon mats and specially designed concrete blocks (turfblocks, monoslabs, shiplap, Lok-Gard, Gobi, Erco, and so on). Some of these are shown in Fig. 7-12.

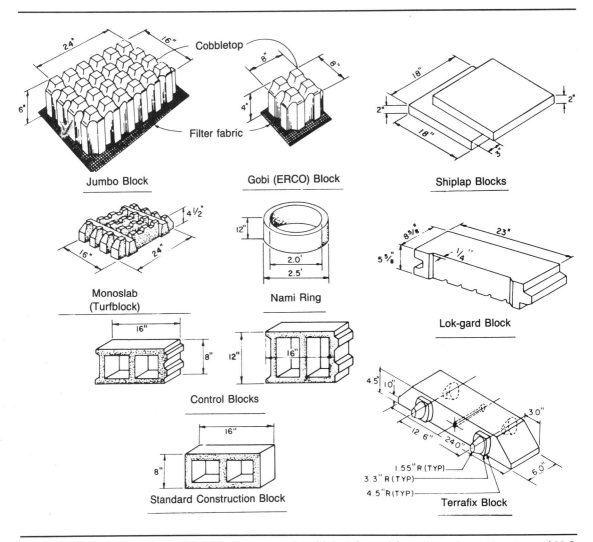

Fig. 7-12. Revetments can be constructed from a variety of prefabricated materials as shown here. (Courtesy of U.S. Army Corps of Engineers.)

Storm Water Drainage Control

For all intents and purposes, the second half of this book begins with this chapter. You'll recall that throughout the earlier discussions of retaining walls, constant mention was made of the need to control drainage to ensure that the wall remained stable. Controlling drainage, whether behind a retaining wall, in a basement, or in the backyard, will be the topic discussed in the next few chapters. Before examining specific drainage problems and possible solutions, it is important that you become familiar with some of the problems surrounding storm and groundwater drainage.

In general, drainage problems can be divided into two categories: surface drainage and subsurface drainage. As their respective names imply, surface drainage refers to water that runs along the top of the ground, while subsurface drainage alludes to underground water. It is extremely important that both forms of drainage be kept under control on every homesite. At best, water running freely across a lot is a nuisance for both you and your neighbors. At worst, uncontrolled drainage can wreak havoc with sloping lots, house foundations, basement walls, existing retaining walls, and utility services, to mention a few potential problem spots.

THE RAINFALL CYCLE

By and large, it is beyond the ability of television weathermen to predict with complete accuracy whether or not it is going to rain. In the same

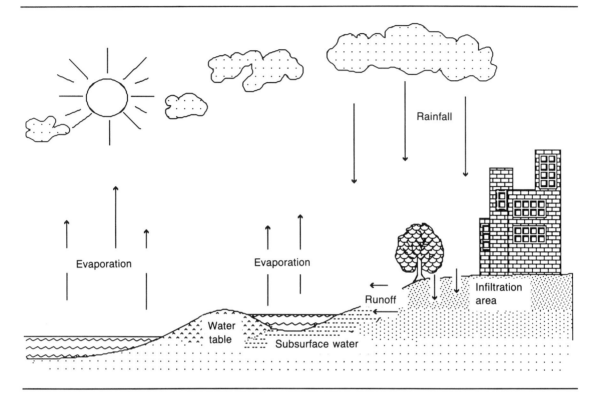

Fig. 8-1. The rainfall cycle.

sense, it is ordinarily impossible for builders to foretell with complete accuracy the effect of water on a building site when it does rain. Nevertheless, it is important for builders to have at least a basic familiarity with the nature of rainfall before they can design and build structures to withstand it.

As you probably learned in elementary school, the rainfall cycle begins with the evaporation of water on the Earth, which forms clouds. Those clouds then produce precipitation, which falls back down to the Earth as shown in Fig. 8-1. There is no way to consistently tell what the short-term characteristics of the cycle will be. A month of heavy rains can be followed by several months of drought. On the other hand, we do know that over the long-term (several consecutive years or decades, for instance), certain weather patterns are evident, and this information can be useful to builders as well as farmers. A certain area, for example, may get an extremely heavy rain once every 10 years. Because houses are generally built to last several decades, builders must plan for those times when heavy rains fall, not for just normal rainfall.

To give you an idea of the possible variations, consider that once every two years, the central part of New Mexico can expect to get a storm that lasts for about an hour and pours about ¾-inch of rainfall. Once every five years, however, the same area can expect a similar 1-hour storm that dumps about 1¼-inch of rain. At least once every 25 years, the same area will be pounded with a 1¾-inch rainstorm, while once every 100 years, a 3-inch storm will occur. If you are a builder in that area, you generally need to plan on building a structure that will withstand the 3-inch rainstorm, even though you may not live to ever see such rain. (Hopefully, houses and walls that we build will last at least 100 years.) You can contact your local U.S. Department of Agriculture office for specific information on the rainfall characteristics where you live.

Rainfall has several basic traits to be considered. Among these characteristics are the length of time it rains, how hard it rains, and how often it rains. Any particular rainstorm can exhibit any or all of these characteristics. Among the generalizations that can be made about rainstorms are that violent storms don't last long, while storms that last a long time and cover a lot of ground usually aren't that intense. The point to remember is that home drainage systems must be designed and built to withstand the worst-case, combined efforts of all three of these rainfall characteristics for any particular locality.

SURFACE DRAINAGE

Surface drainage, commonly referred to as runoff, is water that has not been absorbed into the ground and is in the process of making its way to the nearest low spot. Storm drainage is commonly carried off in channels, pipes, or swales with the intensity of runoff flow depending on a number of things, among them the angle and length of the slope, the type of ground surface, and the presence and type of vegetation.

Although the previous section of this chapter focused on runoff stemming from periodic rainfall, it shouldn't be forgotten that some of the most serious surface drainage problems occur at certain times of the year. In that part of the country in which I now live (Northern California), we get hit with extremely heavy rains starting just before Thanksgiving and lasting on into January. Because the ground quickly becomes saturated with water, it doesn't take long for runoff problems to become horrific. The rest of year, however, surface drainage problems are for the most part nonexistent. For about five years, however, I lived in Canada, where there were even more knotty runoff problems around April as the heavy snow pack melted. Although the source of the problem differs, the problems themselves are the same—how to deal with an extraordinary amount of water that seems to appear quite suddenly.

There are a number of obvious things you can do to the surface of the ground to lessen the negative effect of runoff water. For one thing, some bare or near bare slopes can be planted with groundcover. This will break up the straight-line flow of the water, slowing it down and lessening its intensity in the process. In addition, the root systems of the plants will hold the soil in place so it is less likely to erode. A dense grass or turf can not only slow down the runoff, but can actually absorb some of it as well. Check with your local greenhouse to find out which groundcover that grows in your area has the highest absorption qualities. (This approach may not be as effective if the runoff comes from melting snow, because the ground cover may be underneath the snow.)

You should also examine the ground itself. Clay-based soils do not absorb much water. If you have a slope made up mostly of claylike soils, you can replace some of the topsoil with a more porous material. If it is not practical to replace the entire face of the slope, you can try turning over (plowing) the soil and mixing in some granular material.

One of the most common and most effective runoff control methods is terracing, which involves the construction of long, low mounds of earth that retard and direct water as it runs down the hillside. Terraces are laborious to construct, especially if you dig and shape them by hand. They are, however, effective in most terrains and climates and can carry runoff even when the ground is covered with snow.

While earthen terraces are generally sufficient for gently sloping ground, a series of masonry or wood retaining walls may be necessary to control steep hillsides. Figure 8-2 shows a series of wood retaining walls, while Fig. 8-3 shows a succession of rock walls on the hillside of a lake.

Fig. 8-2. Terraces can be fashioned by building a series of low, wood retaining walls as shown here.

In some instances, terraces are combined with or actually are open channels to carry the water directly to a pond or drain. It is doubtful that you will want to have bare open (concrete lined) channels in your yard, because they are both unattractive and difficult to build. Instead, you'll probably want shallow, soil-based channels that are lined with grass. These are unobtrusive and relatively easy to construct. Additionally, the grass-lined channels can provide extra resistance to erosion. At the same time, however, grass-lined channels need to be significantly wider than a concrete- or stone-lined channel built at the same site. Typical channel linings range from fine sand or silt, which is highly susceptible to erosion, to the aforementioned concrete or hard rock. In between can be coarse sand, gravel, pebbles, and sod which are increasingly resistant to erosion.

There are a number of common shapes for surface drainage channels, as exhibited in Fig. 8-4. Selection of an individual type of channel depends on a number of factors, foremost among them the slope of the watercourse. If the angle of the slope is steep, you'll want to use a channel that slows down the velocity of the water: perhaps a rectangular or parabolic shape with a grass lining. If, however, the slope is gradual and the resulting velocity of the water is relatively slow, you'll probably want to build a triangular channel lined with concrete, clay, or a similar impervious material. This will cause the water to run with a relatively high velocity down the slope being drained.

There are some precise engineering drainage calculations that can be

Fig. 8-3. Masonry terraces can be attractive and functional as shown here. (Photo courtesy of E.W. Dolstein.)

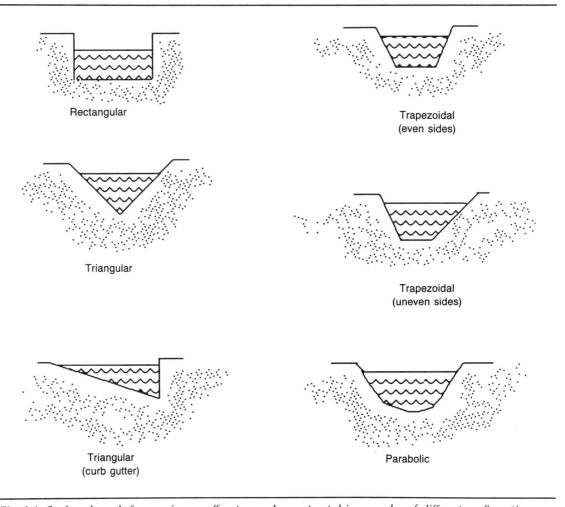

Fig. 8-4. Surface channels for carrying runoff water can be constructed in a number of different configurations.

made to determine the slope of the channel. Such calculations usually express a ratio of the number of feet the slope drops over a linear 1000 feet (or between lines on a contour map). These calculations, however, are generally only necessary when large-scale drainage systems are being constructed, those that drain a housing development or park, for instance. For most backyard do-it-yourself projects, there is usually little need to worry about complicated engineering calculations. If you are concerned about the requirements of a particular job, don't hesitate to call a professional civil engineer.

Also important to the design and construction of drainage channels is the area of the surface that is to be drained. Obviously, the greater the land area, the larger the channel will need to be. Homeowners who are trying to determine surface area most often forget to take into account the roof area of the house itself. Instead, they typically consider only the yard area and neglect the roof of the house. So if you have a large house that takes up most of the yard, base your assumptions on the entire area of the property to be drained, including the house.

Another important factor to be considered is that water coming off the roof is traveling at a greater velocity than the same water running off the yard. This is because the slope of the roof is usually steeper than the yard, the surface of the roof is impermeable, and the runoff is collected into a concentrated pipe (the gutter and downspout) to be discharged at a high velocity. When preparing open drainage channels to carry water away from the house, be sure they are deep enough and wide enough to hold water from the roof. (Rain gutters and roof runoff control will be discussed later in this book.)

SUBSURFACE DRAINAGE

As its name implies, subsurface water is any water which runs beneath—either naturally or artificially—the surface of the ground. Natural underground water flow can stem from Artesian or other wells and springs to high-water tables in low-lying areas. Artificial subsurface water flow may come from storm water drainage conduits or house wastewater pipes. In some instances, natural and artificial subsurface drainage can combine to cause problems.

In my backyard, for instance, there is a buried clay tile drain line which simply picks up excess rain water as it soaks into the ground, carries it out under the sidewalk, and into the street. To help out a neighbor, I dug up the drain and tied a 4-inch flexible pipe into it. He uses it to carry water from a sump pump in his yard. This saves him from having to lay his own conduit or having a garden hose stretched out to the street.

In fact, the 4-inch corrugated polyethylene pipe I used for that drainage conduit (Fig. 8-5) is one of the most common drainage pipes used around houses today. Perforated corrugated plastic pipes have all but replaced the 1-foot long clay tiles that were used by builders for the past 50 years. At the same time, larger diameter unperforated corrugated plastic pipe—those in the range of 12 to 24 inches—have replaced metal corrugated culverts for use under driveways.

Corrugated plastic pipes can be put to a variety of uses by homeowners, farmers, and construction workers. The reasons for the wide acceptance of this drainage material include its low cost, ease of installation, resistance to rust and corrosion, and flexibility. Around the house, corrugated plastic pipes are used for interior and exterior foundation drains, septic tanks, basement and window-well drains, drain-

Fig. 8-5. Corrugated polyethylene pipe is one of easiest-to-work-with and most commonly used subsurface drainage conduit materials used around single-family homes. It comes in a variety of diameters, the most common being 4-inch.

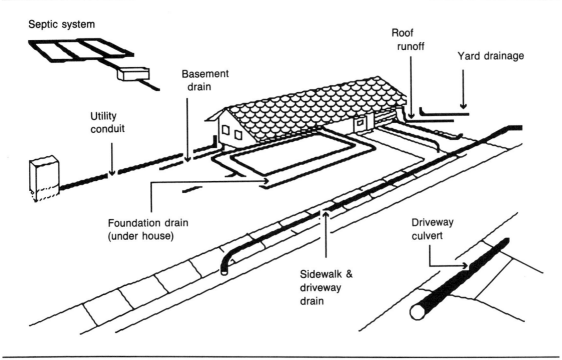

Fig. 8-6. Corrugated plastic pipes are typically used in a variety of applications around the house as shown here.

age under driveway and sidewalks, surface inlets, and as dry conduits for underground utility service. See Fig. 8-6. The rule of thumb is that if the pipe is to be used as a drainage line, perforated tubing (pipes that have small slits cut into them) should be used. This will allow water to enter and leave the pipe anywhere along the line, wherever soil conditions allow it. If the line is intended to transport water away from the house, use solid, non-perforated tubing so that water does not leak out. Additionally, use non-perforated tubing around trees, shrubs, or other plants where roots could enter the tubing and clog up the drain.

When used as exterior foundations drains, the corrugated plastic pipe is installed below the floor level of the house. It channels rainwater and subsurface water away from the footing and foundations in an effort to keep basements dry. Interior foundation drains, on the other hand, are buried on the inside of the foundation (in the crawlspace), and they channel water that normally collects under the house. In the yard, the plastic pipe can be used to carry away water that has collected in low spots. Under driveways and sidewalks, drainage pipes can prevent frost damage and other pavement failures caused by unsettled bases.

Although corrugated polyethylene tubing (3 or 4 inches in diameter) is strong and flexible, it must be installed properly or it will not do an adequate job of providing drainage. For one thing, it is very important that you do not let large clods of dirt or stones rest on or beside the tubing because as the ground settles, the tubing can be crimped or damaged. As much as possible, use gravel or other similar material as the bedding material around the pipe as shown in Fig. 8-7. The bedding material (ideally pea gravel or a mixture of coarse sand and gravel) should completely surround the plastic pipe, being at least 3 inches deep beneath the pipe and another 2 to 3 inches above it. The pipe should be centered in the bedding with at least 4 inches of gravel or other bedding on each side of it. Finally, the bedding should be beneath at least 12 inches of a soil backfill. In summation, the top of the tubing should be no less than 14 inches below the surface of the ground.

The actual depth of the pipe depends on what sort of traffic will travel on the ground above it. If the tubing runs beneath a driveway or other traffic-way, the pipe will need to be buried deeper. For driveways that are intersected by ditches, you will probably need to use a culvert that may be anywhere from 10 to 24 inches in diameter.

Non-perforated plastic culverts are typically stronger but less flexible than plastic tubing, and installing them differs somewhat from the installation of tubing. When digging the trenches to lay culverts in place, the width of the ditch should be twice that of the culvert. An 18-inch culvert, for instance, should be placed in a trench that is at least 36 inches wide, as Fig. 8-8 illustrates. As with tubing, the culvert should be placed in a bedding of gravel or compacted soil, depending on the conditions. Beneath the culvert, the bedding should be a minimum of 6 inches deep, while the minimum thickness of bedding above the culvert is 12 inches. Note that culverts rarely, if ever, have any backfill on top of the bedding

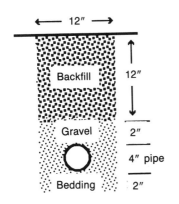

Fig. 8-7. *To provide effective drainage, corrugated plastic pipe must be properly installed as shown here.*

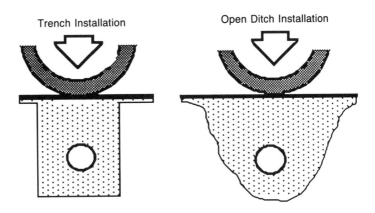

Trench Installation   Open Ditch Installation

Fig. 8-8. Driveway culverts, typically anywhere from 10- to 24- inches in diameter, do not have backfill.

material. If heavy truck or other traffic will go over the culvert, you may want to consider using a corrugated metal culvert. When digging the trench and laying the tubing in it, try to maintain a minimum drop of about ¼-inch over every 10 linear feet of pipe.

ADDITIONAL METHODS OF DRAINAGE CONTROL

In addition to culverts and pipes, there are a number of other synthetic materials that can aid in drainage control, some of which work in conjunction with underground drainage pipes. The most common of these materials is a fine-mesh fabric that can be used both above and below ground. This material has also been adapted for use as a drainage-aid behind retaining walls (see Chapter 4) and along shorelines (see Chapter 7). The problem with these fabrics is that they are sometimes difficult to find. Check with lumberyards or landscaping centers. One manufacturer of this type of material is Mirafi Inc., in Charlotte, NC (for U.S. readers) and in Woodstock, Ontario (for Canadians).

An application for this fabric material is as a *sediment fence*. This fence, which is typically only a couple of feet or so in height, is erected much like any other fence; fence posts must be pounded into the ground and the fencing material stretched between them. The difference, however, is that the fencing material (sometimes called *silt fence*) is an extremely fine-mesh fabric. The fence fabric allows water to flow through but not sediment (see Fig. 8-9). Silt fences are useful when erected at the bottom of slopes and around culverts or storm water drains.

Installation of silt fences is relatively simple, because some fences come pre-assembled: the posts are attached to the fence and simply rolled

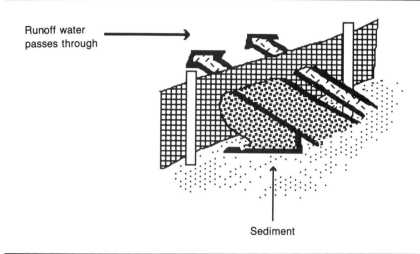

Runoff water
passes through

Sediment

Fig. 8-9. Erosion caused by runoff can be controlled by the installation of fine-mesh silt fences that allow water to pass through, but not sediment.

up in the bundle when you buy it. When you unroll the fencing material, the posts are properly spaced and attached. To start the installation process, it is necessary to dig a small ditch on the up-slope side of where the fence will be. Next, unroll the fence along the down-slope side of the trench and drive the posts into the ground a foot or so deep. Because the fabric won't be fastened to the posts all the way down, take the bottom 6 inches of the material, lay it into the trench, and cover it up with dirt. This will prevent water from running under the fence.

Throughout this book, I have stressed the importance of adequate drainage behind retaining walls and, as Chapter 4 in particular pointed out, the addition of gravel or other coarse aggregate material is essential to ensure proper drainage. The problem with this technique is that the

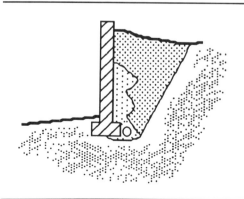

Fig. 8-10. Ditches and retaining walls can also be lined with fabrics to protect the drainage system.

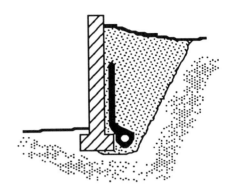

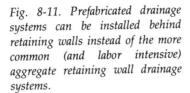

Fig. 8-11. Prefabricated drainage systems can be installed behind retaining walls instead of the more common (and labor intensive) aggregate retaining wall drainage systems.

gravel itself can eventually get choked with silt, negatively affecting drainage. It is possible to use a drainage fabric to protect drainage systems from such build-up. In this case, trenching or other excavation is dug, the trench is lined with silt fence fabric, gravel is put in place, and backfilling is completed, as Fig. 8-10 illustrates. Additionally, the necessity for gravel can be eliminated altogether by the installation of prefabricated drainage structures like that in Fig. 8-11. A main advantage of this procedure is that it reduces to a large degree the weight and pressure exerted on a structural slab.

Yet another type of drainage and erosion control is called a *revegetation mat*. This is a flexible synthetic web which covers the ground, yet allows grass and other natural vegetation to grow through it. In the past, before synthetic mats were available, homeowners commonly used straw or mulch. These natural materials couldn't always control erosion, however, particularly on steep slopes or along the banks of ditches. Because the mats are synthetic, they will not deteriorate like natural mulch, so the mats can be used as a permanent method of erosion control. In addition to holding soil in place, revegetation mats will also retain seed, fertilizer, and immature plants.

To install revegetation mats, grade the site so that it is compact and even. Dig narrow, shallow ditches (sometimes called *check slots*) perpendicular to the slope about every 25 feet. This will help hold the mats in place. Unroll the revegetation mats along the same slant that the water flows. Fix the mat in place using wooden stakes. You can then plant seed and fertilize the ground as normal.

9
CHAPTER

Basement and Foundation Drainage

It is at this point that the distinctions between many of the topics discussed in this book begin to blur. What is the difference, you might ask, between a retaining wall and a basement wall? When does excess runoff cease to be a surface drainage problem and start becoming a subsurface one? How do you distinguish between retaining wall drainage problems and basement wall problems? In truth, there isn't much difference between the problems retaining wall builders face and those confronted by basement/foundation designers. Many of the construction techniques are similar, if not the same.

Probably the biggest difference is not in the actual construction of the wall or drainage system, but in the eventual effect of what happens when things go wrong. If a hillside retaining wall is improperly drained, an inconvenience may occur a few times a year. If a basement wall is improperly drained, however, a homeowner's quality of life can be adversely affected year-round. At best, dampness and mildew may be a problem all the time; at worst, with periodic flooding, the structural integrity of the house itself can be compromised. In this chapter, we'll examine some of the challenges and possible solutions that basement and foundation walls present.

One quick note: many homeowners confuse condensation on basement walls, caused by improper air circulation, with seepage, which is caused by water actually coming through the wall. Condensation occurs when humid air comes in contact with a cold wall, much in the same way that moisture condenses on the side of a glass containing cold water. Obviously, you want to be sure you know the illness before applying a cure. In other words, if the problem with your basement is condensation, you don't want to waste your time on efforts designed to fix seepage problems (and vice versa).

It is actually quite easy to determine whether the moisture in your basement is caused by condensation or seepage. To figure this out, simply tape (on all four edges) a 1-foot square piece of aluminum foil to the basement wall. Then leave the foil there for several days before removing and examining it. If the side of the foil that touches the wall (the bottom side) is damp or wet, the moisture seepage is due to water seeping through the wall. If the surface of the foil that faces you (the top side) is damp, condensation is the source of the problem. If both sides of the foil are wet, then you have both a seepage and a condensation problem.

Condensation problems are relatively easy to correct. Just open some basement windows to provide cross ventilation or install a dehumidifier or exhaust fan. Seepage problems are somewhat more difficult to control and are discussed later in this chapter.

EXTERIOR PROBLEMS AND SOLUTIONS

One house I lived in several years ago had a severe crack running down the basement wall, starting at the top of the wall and down almost to the floor. Although awful to look at, the crack didn't seem to present any immediate danger to the structure of the house. The house was over 40 years old, and it was built on level and stable ground. The crack did become a problem during heavy rains, however. At those times, water simply poured through it into the basement. My initial reaction was to attempt to patch the crack from the inside using, at various times, mortar and caulking. Neither worked. I then looked into digging up the backfill and patching it from the outside. This would have been best, but it would have meant tearing off the front porch, a job that I really wasn't ready to undertake.

While walking along the outside of the house—along the foundation wall—I finally realized that the solution was both obvious and simple. The ground, as I said, was level and stable. The only soil settling that had occurred over the previous 40 or so years had been along the foundation, where the backfill had been added. Consequently, the ground was flat going up to the wall but, underneath the porch and directly above the crack in the basement wall, it was actually depressed. What I did was simply take a few yards of dirt and build up the height 10 or 12 inches along the perimeter of the foundation (including under the porch). I gradually sloped the dirt away from the wall about 6 feet so that a relatively unnoticeable incline existed. From then until the time I

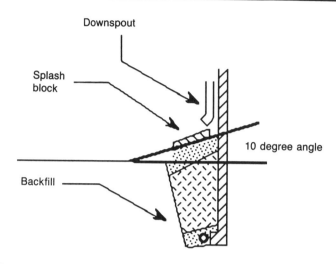

Downspout

Splash
block

10 degree angle

Backfill

Fig. 9-1. A 10-percent backfill grade should be considered the minimum for most houses. This means that the backfill can be about 8 to 10 inches higher than the rest of the yard, extending about 6 feet from the wall.

eventually sold the house, I never experienced water coming through the crack, even in the heaviest rains.

This example underscores two things: one of the most common causes of leakage and moisture in basements is insufficient site drainage; and, the simplest solutions are often the best. It is important that the ground slope away from the foundation of the house. If, over the years, the backfill settles (as in my case), you must be sure to build it back up. (There's no doubt in my mind, especially after digging around the foundation of that house, that the backfill material wasn't properly compacted and probably contained wood scraps or other materials which deteriorated and left airspaces that contributed to excessive settling.)

What kind of grade should there be leading away from or up to the basement/foundation wall? In general, a 10-percent slope should be considered the minimum. This translates to about 8 to 10 inches (high) of fill extending slightly more than 6 to 8 feet away from the house as shown in Fig. 9-1. Make sure the backfill is compacted and check it for settlement after heavy rains (or no less than once a year). Also be sure that your roof drainage—gutters and downspouts—directs water away from the house. Don't let the downspout simply drop the water at the foundation. If this is the case, add conduits or ditches to move it away. (Gutters and downspouts will be discussed in the next chapter.)

If you are planning on building a house, you should consider drainage issues during the initial design stages, especially for homes built on

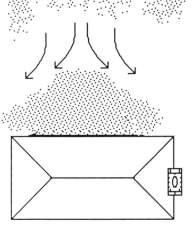

When house sets at the bottom of
a downslope, the natural flow of
runoff can be countered by constructing
an opposing downslope from the house

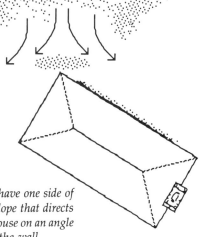

When house is at the bottom of
a downslope, runoff can be diverted
by building the house at an angle
to natural flow of the run-off

Fig. 9-2. When building a house on the downslope side of a hill, don't have one side of the house perpendicular to the runoff unless you also provide a graded slope that directs the water away from the foundation. Another solution is to position the house on an angle to the runoff so that the water doesn't get a chance to stagnate along the wall.

the downside of a slope. The main thing to avoid is positioning the house so that water can run up against it and settle along the foundation wall, as shown in Fig. 9-2. Instead, as this illustration also shows, try to build the house so that a corner faces the downslope. This will, in effect, divide and conquer the runoff by not providing it with an opportunity to run up directly against the wall. If it isn't possible to angle the house and it must directly face the slope, provide a triangular-shaped grade (also as shown) to deflect the runoff and keep it away from the house.

Improperly laid-out backdrains (refer back to Fig. 4-18 for a description of backdrains) are another problem that often leads to basement/crawlspace leakage. With continuous backdrains, the highest part of the conduit should be below the underside of the basement floor or crawlspace. If not, leakage will probably occur. Unfortunately, there is little you can do, once the house is built, to repair unsuitably installed backdrains other than dig them up and reinstall them or turn to pumps inside the house (as described later in this chapter). If you do have to dig up the backdrain, it is recommended that you install filter fabric to help ensure proper drainage.

When the exterior of the basement or foundation wall is accessible, such as during construction or renovation, waterproofing materials should be applied to seal the wall. There are a number of different types of material, including both concrete-based and asphalt-based (mastic) coatings.

Cement-based coatings are good, because the coating becomes an integral part of the masonry surface, not just a separate layer or coating. It is generally easier and cheaper to apply than mastics, and you do not have to immediately pour in the backfill as with some materials. It is usually applied with a coarse brush or, when mixed with sand, can be applied with a trowel.

The application of layers of water-resistant materials isn't the only type of waterproofing that you can apply to a concrete wall. There are also chemical formulations that, when they come in contact with the alkali in a masonry wall, form an efficient seepage-resistant surface. Coatings such as these supply a hydrophobic barrier that is nonetheless permeable to water vapor. Typically, these coatings combine silane primers with acrylic coatings. The silane finds its way into the pores and capillaries of the concrete. By impregnating the pores with silicon, water and harmful chemicals cannot pass into and through the concrete. It should be noted that this method is both effective and expensive. Because it is usually a one-time cost at the beginning of a house building project, however, it may well be worth the expense in years to come. One company that makes such sealers is Moxie International (Sacramento, CA).

INTERIOR PROBLEMS AND SOLUTIONS

Most of the exterior solutions to basement/crawlspace water problems involve keeping the water on the outside of the house. Those solutions don't help you much once the water has made its way through the wall. In this section, I'll discuss steps you can take when you have water inside the house. (If your house is suffering from severe drainage problems in the basement/crawlspace, it may be impossible to control the problem from the interior. In such cases, you must deal with the problem from the outside, no matter how laborious or expensive it may be. Consider any work done to the interior walls as supplemental to that done on the outside.)

Although the source of the water leak in my house was a crack in my basement wall, another common cause of basement or foundation wall leakage stems from holes caused by form ties in poured concrete walls. (For an example of a form tie, refer back to Fig. 5-9.) Form ties, which are made from metal, sometimes come out when forms are taken down or, when left in place, often rust away. In either case, a hole can exist in the wall that will allow water to seep or run through. Of course, the contractor is supposed to cut back the form ties and patch the holes as part of the job, but that isn't always the case. If you have such holes in your basement or crawlspace wall, you can patch them by cutting back (using wire snips) the metal ties about ⅝-inch (see Fig. 9-3), then filling the hole with mortar. For repairs such as this, use a relatively dry mix. After the mortar has dried, you can waterproof the spot. (Waterproofing material will be described shortly.)

When repairing the holes and cracks found in interior walls, you'll need to enlarge (using a cold chisel) the breach so that it has a wedge-shaped, concave configuration. This holds true for both holes that are dry and those that have water flowing from them. For dry holes, use a stiff mortar that consists of one part cement and three parts fine sand or a two-part epoxy mix.

For holes that have water currently running out of them, use a quick-set hydraulic cement that is especially designed to quickly stop running water. In addition to drying quickly, hydraulic cements also expand during the curing process; this helps to more tightly seal cracks and crevices. One such cement is "Waterplug," made by Thoro Systems (Miami, FL); another is "DryLok Fast Plug," from United Gilsonite Laboratories (Scranton, PA). When mixed with water, quick-set concretes

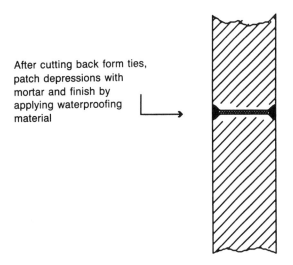

After cutting back form ties, patch depressions with mortar and finish by applying waterproofing material

Fig. 9-3. Form ties that were improperly finished so that water seeps in can be repaired by cutting back the metal tie, patching with mortar, and then waterproofing.

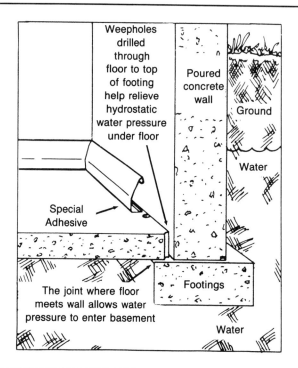

Fig. 9-4. Applying the Basement De-Watering system to a concrete block wall. (Courtesy of Basement De-Watering Systems, Inc.)

set up within 3 to 5 minutes. As the cement is applied, you'll need to use a trowel to hold the cement in place, especially if the water is running with some force. Another way to use the quick-setting cement is to mold it by hand (while wearing latex gloves) into a plug and then force the plug into the previously chiseled hole.

Cement-based waterproofing coatings can be applied to the interior of basement walls. The nice thing about cement-based waterproofing materials is that they "breath" with the wall and therefore do not tend to flake or peel like other coatings. A number of manufacturers make "breathable" coatings, including Thoro Systems, United Gilsonite, and Moxie International. Application of some of the Moxie sealers can be via brush or low-pressure sprayers.

Before application, all cracks, joints, and holes should be repaired using quick-set cement like the one described above. If hydrostatic water pressure has built up behind the wall, you should drill weep holes through the concrete or masonry along the base of the wall. Then apply the waterproofing material to the entire wall surface. When the waterproofing has set at least 24 hours, use a quick-set cement to seal the weep holes. Finally, waterproof the sealed weep holes.

One phenomena which should be mentioned is *efflorescence*, which is a white or light grey stain, powder, or crystal deposit that you often see on masonry basement and retaining walls. This stain is caused by water bringing to the surface of the wall water soluble salts. These salts are naturally present in concrete and cement. In addition to simply looking untidy, the biggest problem with efflorescence is that, unless it is removed, waterproofing paint and other applied coverings will not stick to the surface of the wall, and the wall will continue to leak. Removing the efflorescence requires your washing the wall surface with muriatic acid or a commercially available product—like DryLok Etch—especially designed for such a task. If you undertake a job such as this, follow the directions on the package and be sure to wear rubber gloves and use safety glasses or other eye protection.

Of course, these tactics are still focused on keeping the water out of the basement. Other approaches accept the fact that water will enter the basement/crawlspace, so you might as well control it once it is there. These

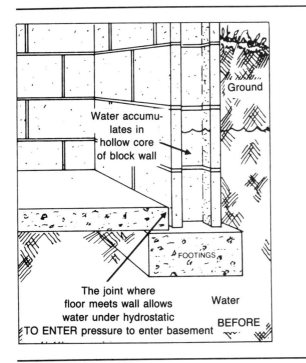
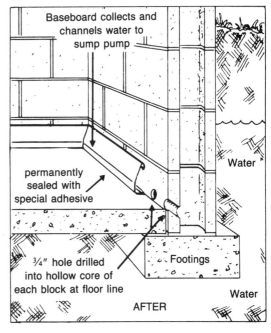

Fig. 9-5. *Applying the Basement De-Watering system to a poured concrete wall.* (Courtesy of Basement De-Watering Systems, Inc.)

techniques generally involve directing the water to a central reservoir, then pumping it out from there.

This is the basic strategy of a company called Basement De-Watering Systems, Inc., (based in Canton, OH, although local dealers are found nationwide). As both Figs. 9-4 and 9-5 suggest, this approach requires that weep holes be drilled through the wall along the base of the interior. A vinyl baseboard is then glued to the wall and floor using a special epoxy sealer. This serves as a drain line which carries the water to a sump pump reservoir as shown in Fig. 9-6.

If you are not familiar with sump pumps, they are a type of pump that are placed at the bottom of a "sump" pit or reservoir. As the pit fills up with water, a float switch automatically turns on the pump, which pumps the water out of the pit. When the water drops to a pre-determined level, the float switch turns the pump off. Sump pits are often about 2 feet in diameter and of depths varying from 1 to 2 feet. There are two types of sump pumps: the pedestal pump, where the electrical motor stands on a pedestal above the water level; and the submersible sump pump, which can actually be covered with water and yet remain

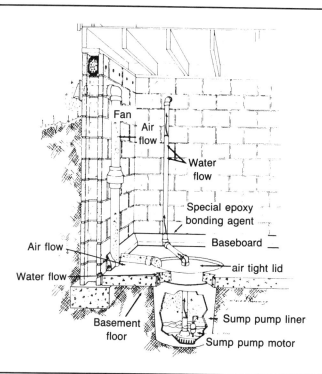

Fig. 9-6. The Basement De-Watering system complete with sump pump. (Courtesy of Basement De-Watering Systems, Inc.)

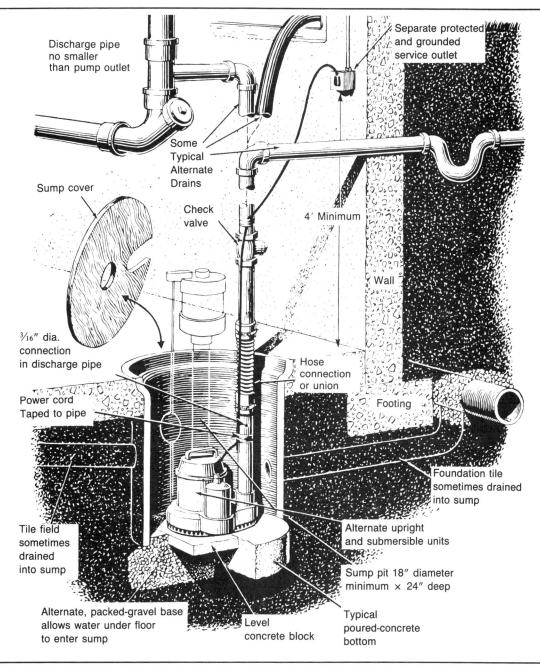

Discharge pipe no smaller than pump outlet

Separate protected and grounded service outlet

Some Typical Alternate Drains

Sump cover

Check valve

4′ Minimum

Wall

³⁄₁₆″ dia. connection in discharge pipe

Hose connection or union

Power cord Taped to pipe

Footing

Tile field sometimes drained into sump

Foundation tile sometimes drained into sump

Alternate upright and submersible units

Sump pit 18″ diameter minimum × 24″ deep

Alternate, packed-gravel base allows water under floor to enter sump

Level concrete block

Typical poured-concrete bottom

Fig. 9-7. An installed sump pump system will look something like this. Note that set up applies to both submersible and pedestal sump pumps. (Courtesy of the Sump and Sewage Pump Manufacturers Association.)

undamaged. Although the submersible pump is more expensive, it is preferred over the pedestal pump because it cannot be damaged by water,
generally requires less maintenance, and easier to handle and install.
Sump pumps can be used both inside and outside the house.

Sump pumps should be installed in the lowest part of the basement
or crawlspace. If you are placing a sump pump in an existing basement,
you may have to knock a hole in the concrete floor; you may also want
to be sure the location is in an inconspicuous location. As mentioned,
the sump pit should not be less than 18 inches in diameter or less than
24 inches deep. You should construct the reservoir from concrete, steel,
plastic, or other such material and add a removable lid.

When placing the pump into the pit, position it in the center of the
pit floor so that the pump or the float switch does not come in contact
with the pit wall. Connect the discharge pipe to the pump and to house
drainage system. If the sump has to pump the water a long way or more
than 6 feet vertically, install a check valve in the discharge pipe. This one-
way valve will keep water from flowing back down the pipe when
pressure lets off. Follow the specific directions provided with the sump
pump for details. Figure 9-7 provides a general description of how an
installed sump pump system should look.

10
CHAPTER

Designing and Installing
Roof Drainage Systems

Many people are surprised to learn that one of the major sources of drainage headaches is not under their feet, but over their heads. In other words, the gutters and downspouts (the main components of a roof drainage system) around the roof of your house can play a big part in determining the well-being of your basement/foundation walls. If not properly designed, the roof drainage system can be a major headache. Considering their importance, it is very surprising that many houses have poorly laid-out and inefficient gutters and downspouts, while many other houses do not have them at all. This is even more surprising considering that gutters and downspouts are relatively inexpensive and easy for most homeowners to install and maintain.

The purpose of gutters is straightforward: the horizontally oriented gutters (called "eavestroughs" in some areas) collect the water running off the roof and channel it to a vertically oriented downspout. The downspout then directs the runoff down the side of the house and away from the foundation. Many people are confused about gutters and downspouts because they are made from a variety of materials (galvanized metal, aluminum, copper, wood, vinyl, etc.), they come in a number of different shapes (half-round, square, etc.), and they have a confusing array of parts (gutter section, elbows, drop outlets, straps, connectors, etc.). But what really scares people about gutters and downspouts is that you must work with them from the top of a ladder, and the heights of many houses makes installation a potentially dangerous job. This is compounded by the fact that gutter sections typically come in 10-foot long segments and, although they are not heavy, they are awkward, especially at the top of a ladder.

DETERMINING ROOF DRAINAGE NEEDS

As mentioned above, gutters are made from a variety of materials. In the past, the most common type of gutters were steel, copper, and wood. For the most part, these are not used much any more, except in special situations, because they typically cost more, are more difficult to install, and they require more maintenance than other alternatives. On the plus side, many people do prefer gutters made from wood, copper, and steel because they look better.

The more commonly preferred gutter material is aluminum and vinyl. I have installed both (as well as wood and galvanized metal) and prefer vinyl, because it is not as susceptible to dents and bending as is aluminum. (I do, however, like better the way that aluminum looks.) Both materials are light-in-weight and easy to cut to fit. For me, the big advantage is that once installed, the maintenance requirements are virtually nonexistent. They don't have to be painted every two or three years like wood or steel. You simply have to ensure that they aren't clogged and that they are fastened securely to the house.

No matter what type of gutter material you decide to work with, it is important to become familiar with all of the different components and their names. Figure 10-1 illustrates these. In most instances, you will need to have a few of just about all of these pieces. Of course, the gutter section itself makes up the biggest part of the system and it, like the downspout, normally comes in sections that are 10 feet in length. The components you'll probably need most of are the hangers (there are several different methods for hanging gutters, each with its own unique hanger). Because it is generally recommended that you have one hanger every 3 or 4 feet, you may need to get several dozen hangers for a typical house.

Guttering material is both cheap and expensive. By this, I mean that the gutters themselves are relatively cheap to buy. I recently re-guttered my house and bought 10-foot sections of vinyl guttering for less than $3.00 each. This was relatively cheap. The other components ended up costing much more money. I paid about $1.80 each for the fascia brackets (hangers), almost $4.00 each for the 90-degree corner pieces (mitres), nearly $3.00 for the joint connectors, almost $7.00 for 10-foot sections of downspouts, and so on. As you can see, the cost of the entire roof drainage system quickly escalated, although the gutters themselves were relatively inexpensive.

Gutters usually come in widths of 4, 5, or 6 inches. The width you need is determined by the area (square footage) of the roof. A house with a 700- to 800-square-foot roof can get by with 4-inch gutters; from 800-

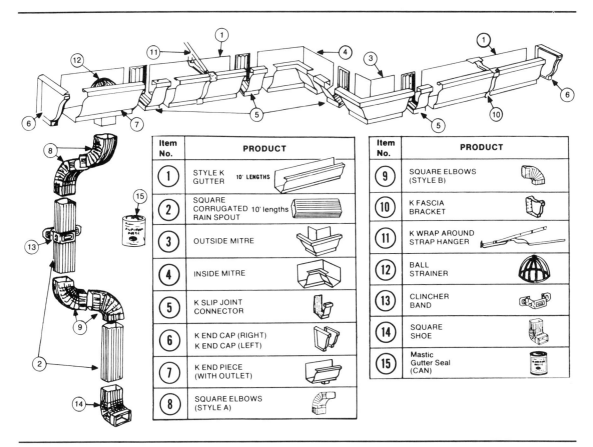

Item No.	PRODUCT		Item No.	PRODUCT	
1	STYLE K GUTTER 10' LENGTHS		9	SQUARE ELBOWS (STYLE B)	
2	SQUARE CORRUGATED 10' lengths RAIN SPOUT		10	K FASCIA BRACKET	
3	OUTSIDE MITRE		11	K WRAP AROUND STRAP HANGER	
4	INSIDE MITRE		12	BALL STRAINER	
5	K SLIP JOINT CONNECTOR		13	CLINCHER BAND	
6	K END CAP (RIGHT) K END CAP (LEFT)		14	SQUARE SHOE	
7	K END PIECE (WITH OUTLET)		15	Mastic Gutter Seal (CAN)	
8	SQUARE ELBOWS (STYLE A)				

Fig. 10-1. Components that make up a roof drainage system.

to 1500-square-foot, 5-inch-wide gutters should be used; and for houses larger than 1500-square-foot, 6-inch-wide gutters are required.

The guidelines for determining how much gutter and downspout you need are pretty much the same for all gutter types. To begin, measure the length of the eaves of your house and add up the total. Divide total length by 10 to see how many gutter sections you'll need. Multiply this number by 3 to find out how many hangers you'll need. (Note that there are different kinds of hangers, including strap hangers, fascia brackets or clips, and long spikes with spacer tubes.) Next, count the number of inside and outside corners that gutters must wrap around. (You'll need an appropriate corner for each.) Because you should have at least one downspout for every 35 feet of gutter, determine the number of drop outlets (also referred to as "end pieces with outlets.") For every point where a gutter section terminates, you'll need an end piece (note that end pieces come in both left- and right-hand configurations, depending on which side the gutter terminates). Finally, you'll need one slip-joint connector for every place two gutter sections meet, where a gutter meets a drop outlet, or where a gutter meets a corner (inside or out). That takes care of the gutter.

For each downspout, you'll need at least three elbows and enough 10-foot downspout sections to reach from the eaves to the ground. Furthermore, you'll need extra downspout sections as miscellaneous pieces to connect the elbows; the amount depends on your particular configuration. You'll also need at least one downspout strap (also called a *clincher band*) for every 6 feet of downspout. You should plan on using one of the elbows at the bottom of the downspout so that the water does not just dump straight down at the foundation. This elbow should empty the water out onto a concrete splash block or should run into a conduit or another section of downspout. If at all possible, the water should be directed so that it diffuses at a point about 10 feet from the foundation wall.

INSTALLING GUTTERS

One of the most difficult aspects of installing gutters is making sure that they maintain a consistent and suitable slope towards the downspouts. A recommended slope is ½-inch for every 10 feet of gutter (or 1 inch for every 20 feet). In cases where the run of gutter exceeds 35 or 40 length between downspouts, it is best to fix a high point at the midpoint and slope the gutter towards both ends. Don't assume that the roof and eaves are accurately sloped; sometimes eaves bend, especially at the corners of the house. Use a level to determine whether or not the roof is level, then drive a nail into the highpoint or where the gutters will be. Measure out 10 feet, drop down a ½-inch, and drive another nail in place. Start at the second nail and repeat the procedure for the next run of gutter. (The third nail, at the 20-foot mark, should be 1-inch below the first, the fourth nail, at the 30-foot mark, should be 1½-inch below the first.) Use string or chalkline as a guide for positioning the gutter.

Before actually beginning the installation process, it is a good idea to lay out in order on the ground all of the parts for a particular run of gutter. If you have a helper, then that person can simply hand the parts to you as needed. The actual installation process will depend on the type of gutter hangers you will be using. In some cases, the manufacturer of a particular type of guttering material will recommend one type of hanger. I prefer the wrap-around strap hangers because the weight is more evenly distributed. These are designed, however, to be used with composite shingle roofs where the hanging strap that is nailed into the roof can be tucked underneath a shingle. My second preference is for fascia brackets, which are nailed to the fascia or end of the eaves. Vinyl or plastic gutters most often used these. Frankly, I'm not much of a fan of spikes-and-spacers because they tend to pull out and because the large spikes sometimes split the wood. They also require you to drill holes in the gutter to drive the spikes through, which is extra work and can lead to dented or bent gutters.

One important task is to adequately seal all of the points where gutter components overlap and meet: at gutter connectors, or where the gutter section meets the drop outlet, for instance. This is typically done as you go. Use mastic gutter seal or caulking. If you don't seal the gutter properly, there's not much use in having it there in the first place.

INSTALLING DOWNSPOUTS

Downspouts carry the water from the gutter (via the drop outlet) down to the ground. Installation of the downspouts is relatively straightforward, with any peculiarities stemming from the characteristics of the job at hand. The most difficult part of the installation process is configuring the elbows like that shown in Fig. 10-2.

As mentioned before, the most important part of the downspout isn't at the top—it is at the bottom. You must make sure that the water is carried away from the foundation wall, or there isn't much point in going to the trouble of putting up the guttering in the first place. If you don't particularly want to have a section of downspout or conduit stretched out across the yard, you may want to consider burying a plastic pipe underground and directing the runoff to a sewer drain, a dry well (typically constructed by digging a large hole in the ground, filling it with large rocks, then covering it over again), or in a herringbone drainage pattern. Whatever your solution is, don't release the water from the downspout until it is 10-feet from the house or unless it drains from the downspout onto a discernible slope.

ROOF DRAINAGE MAINTENANCE

Maintaining an existing roof drainage system is not difficult and generally involves simple periodic cleaning. More than anything else, two conditions lead to the necessity for cleaning. If your house is surrounded by tall trees with leaves that fall onto the roof, you'll probably need to clean them out of the gutters several times a year. Otherwise, they clog up the downspout and gutter and lessen the effectiveness of the system. This problem can be alleviated by the installation of *leaf guards* that slip under the shingles but over the top of the gutters. These prevent large leaves from getting into the gutter, yet allow water to run off into the trough. You might also need to insert ball or wire strainers over or into the entrance of the downspout hole. Such a device will catch leaves before they go down the downspout and clog it up at the elbows. (When a

Fig. 10-2. Elbow configuration is one of the most difficult aspects of downspout installation because there are several different types of component parts that must be aligned.

downspout does get clogged up, simply run a plumber's or electrician's snake or a running water hose down the downspout to clear it out.)

The second cleaning that needs to be performed involves the removal of sandlike roofing substances from the gutters. This is usually a problem only with composite shingled roofs. There is no easy way to prevent the roofing material from washing off into the gutter and no really easy way to clean it out. You simply have to scoop it out into a bucket and then wash out the gutter. You must clean this material out because it adds excessive weight to the gutters and can impede the flow of water.

The caulking of all gutters should be checked every year or so for leaks. If leaks occur, caulking or mastic should be applied to stop them. Joints in wooden gutters should be caulked on a yearly basis no matter what, and they should be painted (inside and out) every other year whether the rest of the house needs it or not.

If you live in those parts of the country that experience brutal winters, you know that ice and snow can play havoc with gutters. This is particularly a problem with houses that have low-pitched roofs. Ice build-up just above the gutters can cause severe damage to the house, not just with the extra weight, but because melting snow and ice can actually find its way down inside the walls. When I lived in Canada, one house in particular kept getting melting water between the exterior and interior walls of the house. To stop this, I had to climb up on the roof throughout the winter and break away the ice dams all along the perimeter of the roof. An easier solution is to simply install a weatherproof electrical tape along the eaves of the roof. The tape will heat up and melt the ice whenever it builds up. Melting snow and ice, which slides down the roof, can also tear off gutters. To prevent damage to the drainage system, you can install special snow guards, which should be available in lumberyards or hardware stores in areas where this is a problem.

Glossary

accretion—The natural accumulation of sand and other aggregate along a beach.

aggregate—Concrete formed by the mixing of cement, sand, gravel, and water.

backfill—The process and material used to fill a void created by construction.

backfill pressure—The pressure exerted on a wall by the fill material added after construction.

backhoe—A tractor with an attached hydraulic-powered bucket/shovel, used for excavation.

beach—A sand or gravel area between water and the first permanent vegetation along the edge of the water.

bed joint—The mortar used as a horizontal base for bricks, concrete blocks, natural stone, etc.

bluff—A high, steep soil bank at the edge of the water.

brick—A rectangular, clay-based masonry block used for construction.

bulkhead—A wall that protects the shore from the force of waves.

butter—To apply mortar to a brick or block.

cap—(1.) To apply a finish material along the top of a wall. (2.) The finish material placed along the top of a wall. The cap also prevents water from seeping into the wall.

caulking—A material used to fill joints in a structure.

cement—A material that adheres masonry building blocks to each other, consisting of a mixture of silica, alumina, and lime. Hydration occurs when cement is mixed with water. This process produces the adhesion. *See* concrete.

check valve—A valve that allows water to flow in only one direction. Used with sump pumps to keep water from going back down into the pit.

clay—A fine-grained soil made up of particles that are less than 0.00015 inch in diameter.

concrete—A mixture of cement, sand/gravel, and water, used to adhere masonry building blocks. Common mixture ratios are 10 percent cement, 20 percent water, and 70 percent aggregate.

condensation—Excessive dampness in the basement or crawlspace caused by inadequate air circulation.

contractor—A person who signs an agreement to perform a certain job. Contractors are generally licensed by State governments. *See* general contractor and subcontractor.

course—A layer of bricks, blocks, or stone.

crawl space—The low space beneath the floor of a house which provides access for utilities. Typically, the crawl space has not been excavated deep enough to be finished as a basement.

curing—The process that concrete goes through as it slowly dries. Mortar takes about 4 days to cure; retaining walls require 7 or more days.

cut and fill—The removal and/or addition of soil during the excavation process.

deadman—An anchor attached to a wall, and buried underground and behind the wall, that helps keep the wall from falling away from the hill.

drainage—The process water goes through as it goes from a high point to a lower one.

efflorescence—White or light grey salt deposits that collect on the exterior face of a masonry wall. The soluble salts are naturally found in cement and concrete and are brought to the surface by excessive moisture. Efflorescence must be removed using muriatic acid or similar material before paint or waterproofing material will adhere to the masonry.

elevation—A straight-on drawing showing how an exterior wall of a house would look if you were looking directly at it. A house normally can be seen from four elevations.

epoxy cement—A fast-drying cement made from a mixture of sand, epoxy, and cement.

estimate—A preliminary view of the cost of a job.

erosion—The process of natural forces wearing away the land.

equivalent fluid method—A means of determining backfill pressure on a retaining wall.

fill—Materials such as earth, clay, gravel, or sand that are added to an area to increase the local elevation. In almost all cases, fill must be compacted.

filter cloth—Synthetic material designed to allow water to pass through, but not soil.

floodwall—A barrier of water-resistant material (concrete, for instance) designed to keep water away from a building.

footing—Poured concrete that supports the wall and spreads the load of the wall so it does not exceed the soil bearing capacity. The footing is usually wider than the foundation and beneath the frost line. Typically from 6 to 12 inches thick.

frost line—The depth at which frost will not normally penetrate; usually from 6 to 12 inches deep.

general contractor—On-site job manager, who must ensure that the project runs on schedule.

gravel—Small granules of rock with diameters ranging from 0.18 to 3 inches.

groundwater—Natural water below the surface of the ground.

hydrostactic loads—Forces put upon a wall surface by water. The pressure increases with the square of the water depth.

lateral earth pressure—Horizontal forces exerted by the soil against a vertical structure.

masonry—A building trade that specializes in masonry materials such as stones, blocks, or bricks.

mortar—A mixture of cement, water, and sand. Mortar differs from concrete in that aggregate (gravel) is not used. Common mixtures are 3 parts sand, 1 part masonry cement, and enough water to make the mixture workable. Mortar typically is not as strong as concrete.

overturning—The process of a retaining wall being pushed by the soil from behind and at the top of the wall.

perc test—A test to determine the ability of the soil to absorb discharged waste water: percolation.

permeability—The property of rock or soil that enables water to pass through it.

pier—A vertical support member that is driven into the ground by mechanical means and is supported by friction between the pier and the surrounding earth.

plan view—A drawing of a structure looking down from above.

plan check—The process whereby the building department inspects the construction plans prior to granting a building permit.

plot plan—A graphic description of a parcel of land, usually compiled by a licensed surveyor.

pier and beam—Of or referring to a foundation that consists of individual vertical piers connected by horizontal beams that support the floor system.

pilasters—Rectangular or columnar supports that shore up walls; differ from triangular-shaped buttresses.

plumb—Vertically straight.

prime contractor—The job-site manager who usually hires subcontractors. *See* general contractor.

PVC—Polyvinyl chloride. A corrosion-resistant plastic material used to make pipe or protect metal.

rebar—An abbreviation for metal reinforcement bars.

retaining wall—Any wall constructed to withstand the lateral forces of the soil.

revetment—A stone facing applied to a slope in order to fight erosion.

rip-rap—Broken stones or rubble put on slopes to inhibit erosion or scouring. Primarily used along shorelines where wave action can erode the land.

runoff—Water that goes along the surface of the ground.

sand—Granular soil with particles between 0.003 and 0.18 inches in diameters.

scouring—The erosion of soil by velocity runoff.

seawall—A wall that separates land and water. *See* bulkhead.

seepage—Moisture that percolates through a wall. Not to be confused with condensation.

setback requirement—The minimum distance a structure must be from a property line.

slope—The relationship between the vertical rise and horizontal distance of an embankment.

stucco—An exterior wall finish consisting of cement, sand, lime, and water and held in place by reinforcement wire.

subcontractor—A building specialist hired to complete a single, limited phase of the construction process.

terraces—A series of manmade, horizontally level platforms that provide relatively horizontal surfaces on a hillside.

topographical plat—A drawing illustrating the contours and surface of a plot of land.

topography—The study of a surface configuration.

tuck pointing—To touch-up or repair a wall with mortar.

variance—An exception to a zoning rule.

watershed—An area that drains to a single point.

weep hole—A hole through wall used to keep water pressure from building up behind the wall.

zoning—Of or referring to local regulations that govern the use and application of specific land areas.

Index